IMAGES
of Aviation

COMET AND NIMROD

Comet C2 XK671 on a test flight from Hatfield in 1956, shortly before delivery to 216 Squadron at RAF Lyneham, where it was named *Aquila*. Initially, it was part of the BOAC order for Comet 2s, and allotted registration G-AMXG. However, it was not finished before the BOAC contract was cancelled and was subsequently completed as a Comet C2 for the RAF, flying for the first time on 16 July 1956.

IMAGES
of Aviation

COMET AND NIMROD

Ray Williams

TEMPUS

Tempus Publishing Limited
The Mill, Brimscombe Port,
Stroud, Gloucestershire, GL5 2QG

ISBN 0 7524 1752 5

Typesetting and origination by
Tempus Publishing Limited
Printed in Great Britain by
Midway Clark Printing, Wiltshire

Nimrod MR2P XV241 of the Kinloss Wing, with BOZ counter measure dispenser pods mounted under the wings, flying over the Firth of Forth. The Forth Road Bridge can be seen under the nose of the aircraft and the old railway bridge, just behind the tail.

Contents

Acknowledgements

While compiling this book I received a great deal of assistance, from many organizations and individuals, with information and photographs, for which I am extremely grateful.

I should particularly like to thank Gordon G. Bartley, Barry Guess and Tim Poulton of BAE Systems (formerly British Aerospace), Andrew Siddons of Rolls-Royce, Dawn McNiven of RAF Kinloss, Squadron Leader D.J. Middleton of the Inspectorate of Flight Safety (RAF), Squadron Leader J. Lawson of 201 Squadron and Flight Lieutenant Jane Crowther of 206 Squadron.

I would also like to thank the following: Barry Abraham, Gary Barber, Gordon Brice, Tony Buttler, Wing Commander Derek Collier Webb, Darryl Cott, Scott Henderson, Harry Holmes, Derek James, George Jenks, Ian Lowe, Eric Morgan Jim Morrow, Jim Norval, Phil Pickwick, Rod Smith, Grenville Williams and the Public Relations staffs of Mexicana, Saudia and Singapore Airlines.

Ray Williams
Lymm
June 2000

The first prototype Comet, bearing class B condition markings G-5-1, on a test flight from Hatfield, shortly after it had made its first flight on 27 July 1949. By the time it had appeared at the Farnborough Air Show in September 1949 it had received its civil registration G-ALVG.

Introduction

DH106 Comet

By the beginning of the Second World War in 1939 the British aircraft industry was already fully involved in the design and manufacture of warplanes for the rapidly expanding Royal Air Force and Royal Navy, to the detriment of civil aircraft. This quickly led to the civil aircraft industry in the United States gaining a significant lead over the rest of the world, as it did not join the war until 1941, with excellent transport aircraft like the Douglas DC3 Dakota and its big brother the four-engined DC4 (C54).

When, by the beginning of 1942, confidence in Britain began to grow of a successful conclusion to the war, a committee was formed to consider transport conversions of military aircraft for possible civil use. This committee was therefore responsible for various aircraft such as the York and Lancastrian, developed from the Avro Lancaster, the Halton from the Handley Page Halifax and the Sandringham from the Short Sunderland. Late in 1942 the committee was reconstituted under the chairmanship of Lord Brabazon of Tara to advise the British government of the types of aircraft that would be required as civil transports following the war. The initial report of the Brabazon Committee, submitted to the government in February 1943, proposed five requirements that were to lead to the Bristol 167 Brabazon, the Airspeed AS57 Ambassador, the Vickers 630 Viscount, the Avro 688 Tudor, the Armstrong Whitworth AW55 Apollo, the de Havilland DH104 Dove and the DH106 Comet. The Brabazon No.4 requirement was for a jet-propelled mailplane for the North Atlantic, able to carry a cargo of one ton at a cruising speed of 400mph.

Subsequently, the Brabazon Committee prepared draft specifications for the types that they had initially proposed, which were circulated around the industry for firms to submit tenders, so that the Ministry of Aircraft Production (MAP) could select the companies who would receive contracts to design and develop the various project.

Although a number of the projects considered the use of turboprop engines, only the No.4 requirement specified the use of turbo-jet engines. Initially, very little data was available on the performance of turbojet engines, but by mid-1944 there was sufficient for the committee to realize that with the turbojet engines available at the time, it was not feasible for a turbojet transport to fly the Atlantic. The requirement was changed for an aircraft for Empire and European services carrying fourteen passengers at 450mph at 30,000ft over a range of 800 miles. Before the end of 1944 the de Havilland Aircraft Company had been selected to develop the jet transport. However, before then de Havilland had already formed a design team, under the leadership of R.E. Bishop, which had already started to prepare some initial schemes on a jet transport. One of

Ronald E. Bishop, de Havilland's chief designer, was in charge of Comet design. After starting his career as an apprentice at de Havilland's in 1921 he took charge of design in the late 1930s with the DH95 Flamingo, de Havilland's first stressed skin, all metal aircraft being his first design. During the Second World War he was responsible for the design of the superb DH98 Mosquito.

the earliest of these was a relatively small twin-boomed aircraft powered by three Halford H2 turbojets (later to become the DH Ghost) located in the rear of the fuselage, which was capable of carrying six passengers between London and New York. Other projects included one with a canard layout and another had a tailless aircraft with swept back wings.

During 1944 the MAP issued specification number 20/44 for a jet propelled civil transport; de Havilland allocated number DH106 to the project. The initial design work concentrated on a tailless aircraft with swept back wings, powered by four 5,000lb thrust turbojets buried in the wing roots. A pressurized 8ft diameter fuselage was to have accommodated twenty-four passengers.

To obtain data on the behaviour of tailless aircraft the MAP agreed to the conversion of two DH100 Vampires into experimental, tailless aircraft, to specification E.18/45, as a means to 'conducting full scale experiments into the possibilities of high-speed flight using sweptback wings, obtaining quantitive measurements of aerodynamic and structural phenomena under such conditions, and to act as an approximately half-scale version of a projected multi-engined jet propelled transport aircraft'. The MAP placed a contract with de Havilland in December 1945 for two experimental, tailless aircraft, which were identified by the company as the DH108. Later, the order was increased to five, but in the event only three were completed. The first DH108 TG283 made its maiden flight on 15 May 1946, with the chief test pilot Geoffrey de Havilland Jr at the controls. Unfortunately, he was killed on 27 September 1946 when TG306, the second DH108, broke-up over the Thames Estuary when he was practising for an attempt on the World Speed Record. John Cunningham was promoted as his successor. Although TG283 was restricted to subsonic operation and used for stability, control and landing trials, the second TG306 and the third VW120 were modified for supersonic flight. The VW120, flown by John Derry, became the first British aircraft to exceed Mach1 during a flight on 9 September 1948.

Although the DH108 flight programme provided much useful data the company had already, before the first flight of the DH108 it had come to the conclusion that a tailless aircraft involved an unnecessarily high level of technical risk and therefore the design was changed to include a sweptback tailplane. This new design provided the basis of specification number 22/46, issued in 1946 by the Ministry of Supply (MOS) successor to the MAP, and followed this up later in the year with a contract for two prototype DH106s. Before production of the prototypes started, the design was further changed. The sweepback of the wings was reduced from forty to twenty degrees, an unswept tailplane was introduced and the fuselage diameter was increased to 9ft 9in, which allowed four abreast seating, increasing the passenger seating capacity to thirty-two. The Halford-designed de Havilland Ghost, a centrifugal turbojet engine, was selected for the early aircraft, mainly because of its relatively advanced stage of development, but consideration was already being given to the axial-flow Rolls Royce AJ65 turbojet, which was to become the Avon.

On 21 January 1947 de Havilland received an Instruction to Proceed (ITP) from the MOS for the production of eight DH106 airliners for BOAC, the first production order ever to be placed for a jet airliner. Shortly afterwards, six DH106s were ordered for British South American Airways (BSAA).

Construction of the DH106 prototypes started at Hatfield, under a veil of secrecy, in 1947. In December 1947 de Havilland revived the name Comet for the DH106. The name had previously been used for their twin-engined DH88 racing monoplane that had been successful during the 1930s, particularly when G-ACSS won the MacRobertson England to Australia Air Race in 1934. As construction of the prototypes continued into 1948, various test programmes were carried out, which included flight testing power-operated controls in a DH103 Hornet and a DH108 and fitting a Comet-shaped nose on a Horsa glider TL348, which was towed by a Handley Page Halifax and was used to assess the pilots view and the effects of rain. The DH Ghost engine had run for the first time on 2 September 1945 and air testing commenced on 24 July 1947, with Ghosts installed in the outer nacelles of the Avro Lancastrian VM703. For high altitude trials a Ghost engine was installed in a DH100 Vampire TG278 that had a reinforced cockpit canopy and each wing tip extended by 4ft, enabling de Havilland's chief test pilot John Cunningham to establish a world altitude record of 59,446ft on 23 March 1948.

Early in 1948 the MOS considered that high speed bomber development of the Comet could be useful insurance against the failure of the Avro and Handley Page projects being developed to specification B.35/46. These projects, which became the Vulcan and Victor, were at the leading edge of technology and consequently their programmes carried a high technical risk. Both, however, proved highly successful and gave long and excellent service to the RAF. The de Havilland company was invited to tender and their project, identified as the DH111, made use of many of the Comet components, but with a completely redesigned fuselage. The DH111 was designed to carry a bomb load of 10,000lb, have a range of 3,720 nautical miles and cruise at 450 knots at an altitude of 42,500ft. The DH111 was rejected by the MOS in October 1948, because they considered it to be too small to carry all the equipment, like electronic counter measures, that would be necessary if it entered service, without a significant reduction in fuel load and the unacceptable related reduction in range. Prototypes of the Vickers Valiant and the Short Sperrin were ordered instead of the DH111. The Valiant was the only one to be ordered into protection and subsequently enter service with the RAF.

The first prototype Comet (c/n 06001) totally devoid of markings and in its natural metal finish made its first appearance outside the factory at Hatfield in April 1949, when it was towed out for engine runs. Although advanced looking for its time, its layout was relatively conventional, being a low wing monoplane with moderately swept-back wings, four Ghost engines buried in the wing centre section and unswept tail surfaces. The retractable undercarriage comprized a two-wheel nose undercarriage that retracted rearwards into a bay

De Havilland's original Comet, the DH88, twin-engined, monoplane racer of 1934. F-ANPY, first flew as G-ACSR, flown by Owen Cathcart-Jones and Ken Waller came fourth in the MacPherson Robertson race from England to Australia in October 1934, which was won by another DH88 Comet G-ACSS, flown by C W A Scott and T C Black. The second of a batch of five, G-ACSR was sold to the French Government in April 1935 and was used for experiments relating to high speed air mail services.

under the forward fuselage and large, single wheel main undercarriages that retracted outwards into the wing. The Comet also had the distinction of being the first British airliner to have full-powered flying controls, using a Lockheed servodyne system. Following the success in using Redux bonding in the construction of the DH104 Dove, it was used for the Comet, primarily for fixing top-hat section stringers to the skins, significantly reducing the number of rivets used and consequently the number of holes to be drilled through the outer skin, increasing the strength and reducing weight.

On completion of the functions and tests, the Comet, carrying de Havilland's 'B' condition registration G-5-1, was towed out of the flight shed on 25 July ready to start its flight test programme. The first two days concentrated on taxiing trials, which were progressively developed into high speed runs along the Hatfield runway, during which John Cunningham made three short hops to give him a brief opportunity to experience the feel of the powered flying controls. On completion of the taxiing trials the Comet was given a detailed inspection, before being handed back to the flight crew late in the afternoon of 27 July. John Cunningham decided to proceed with the first flight. With his crew, comprising of himself as captain, J.W. Wilson as second pilot, A.J. Fairbrother as test flight observer, F.T. Reynolds as flight engineer and H. Waters as electrician, he taxied out to the runway. G-5-1 initially made a short hop with full flap, before returning to the end of the runway for its take-off run. The take-off was uneventful, with the Comet leaving the ground in about 500yds, for the start of a successful thrity-five minute first flight of the Comet, the world's first jet-powered airliner. The next flight, on 4 August, was the beginning of an intensive period of test flying, shared by John Cunningham and Peter Bugge, which culminated in the Comet, by then carrying its civil registration G-ALVG, making its first public appearance at the SBAC Air Display at Farnborough at the beginning of September.

Early on the morning of 25 October, G-ALVG was flown by Cunningham from London Heathrow Airport on its first overseas flight to Castel Benito, Libya. After a two hour stay for lunch and refuelling, it returned to London and then on to Hatfield. The 3,000 mile return flight had been covered at an average speed of 448 mph and had been totally trouble free.

December 1949 saw G-ALVG temporarily fitted with two four-wheeled bogies in place of the single main wheel units. These new units would not fit into the existing wheel wells, so they had to be locked in the down position for the flight trials. Although these units were heavier than the original, the general ground handling was found to be far superior and it was therefore decided to adopt these new units for production Comets.

By the end of 1949 other airlines were beginning to take an interest in the Comet. In December Canadian Pacific Airlines (CPA) placed an order for ten Comet 1As, which differed in having an increased fuel capacity, up-rated engines and a passenger capacity of forty-four.

The retractable, single-wheel undercarriage was re-fitted to G-ALVG in February 1950 and immediately the aircraft was involved in a record breaking return flight from Hatfield to Rome, on 16 February, breaking the records in both directions. This was followed on 21 February, with G-ALVG flying with a cabin pressure of 8,000ft at an actual altitude of 40,000ft and further record flights to Copenhagen and Cairo in the Spring of 1950. In April 1950 G-ALVG commenced its tropical trials at Eastleigh, Nairobi in Kenya, completing them at Khartoum in the Sudan. At Khartoum the Comet experienced a problem with its undercarriage, which grounded it for a few days, until a spare part was delivered by BOAC and the aircraft was repaired, enabling the trials to be successfully completed. G-ALVG returned to Hatfield, where it underwent an intensive inspection. By this time, after eleven months, G-ALVG had accumulated some 324 flying hours, without encountering any significant problems.

On 27 July 1950, exactly one year after the maiden flight of the first Comet, the second, carrying the 'B' condition registration G-5-2 (c/n 06002), took to the air for the first time with John Cunningham and Peter Bugge at the controls. This Comet was soon registered G-ALZK and was the first to incorporate the retractable, four-wheel bogie main undercarriage, which had been tested on G-ALVG in December 1949. With two Comets the test flight programme progressed rapidly, with over 1,000 flying hours being achieved by July 1951.

Although the first two Comets were the property of the Ministry of Supply, they were both painted in BOAC colour schemes. On 2 April 1951 G-ALZK was loaned to the BOAC Comet Unit, that had been formed at Hurn, to prepare the airline for the Comet's entry into service. This unit headed, by Captain M.J.R. Alderson, who had spent the previous few months on liaison duties with de Havilland at Hatfield, carried out a programme of some 500 hours of route-proving and crew training, which included flights to Johannesburg, Delhi, Singapore and Djakarta.

When G-ALZK was handed back to de Havillands at Hatfield in October 1951, the number of Comets on order had increased to forty-five, with the Royal Canadian Air Force, Air France, Union Aeromaritime de Transport (UAT) joining BOAC and CPA as customers and many other airlines were beginning to show a great deal of interest in the Comet. All the early export orders were for the improved Comet 1A. BOAC's early interest in a Comet powered by axial flow engines led to the MOS ordering a single prototype identified as the Comet 2X. This aircraft was the sixth Comet 1 (c/n 06006) modified on the production line to take four 6,500lb static thrust Rolls Royce Avon RA9 Mk 501 engines in place of the de Havilland Ghosts.

The first production Comet G-ALYP (c/n 06003) flew for the first time on 9 January 1951 and was followed by three more BOAC aircraft before the end of the year. Only relatively

The first three Comet 2 fuselages under construction at Hatfield in January 1953. These three Comets G-AMXA, G-AMXB and G-AMXC were part of the order of eleven of the Rolls-Royce Avon-powered Comet 2s for BOAC. Although these aircraft had made their first flights between August and November 1953, they were never delivered to BOAC, but were subsequently converted to Comet C2s for the RAF.

minor changes were introduced on the production Comets as a result of the test flight programme. These included a slight increase in the size of the rudder to improve control during a cross-wind take-off, and the introduction of wing fences to improve stall characteristics.

G-ALYP was formally handed over to BOAC on 8 April 1952, by which time it had been issued with an unrestricted Certificate of Airworthiness, the first ever issued for a jet powered aircraft. Prior to its official hand over, G-ALYP had been used for simulated passenger flights to Johannesburg, carrying only freight. Then at 3p.m. on 2 May 1952 G-ALYP, commanded by Captain Alistair Majendie and with a full load of thirty-six passengers, taxied out to inaugurate the world's first commercial jet airliner service. After stops to refuel at Rome, Beirut, Khartoum, Entebbe, and Livingstone, G-ALYP finally touched down at Johannesburg, the end of the route $23\frac{1}{2}$ hours after leaving London. The Comet had achieved star status with the media. This was further enhanced when Queen Elizabeth the Queen Mother, Princess Margaret, Sir Geoffrey and Lady de Havilland made what could only be described as a pleasure flight around Europe on 23 May 1952.

BOAC steadily extended its services and, by August, it had introduced a regular service between London and Ceylon (now Sri Lanka). On 14 October services were further extended to Singapore and, on 3 April 1953, a regular scheduled service was inaugurated on the 10,200 mile London-Tokyo route. The Comet proved a great success with passengers and BOAC achieved load factors of the order of ninety percent, cutting flying times by half.

All nine of BOAC's Comet 1s were completed before the end of 1952. The first of two Canadian Pacific Airlines Comet 1As, CF-CUM (c/n06013), made its maiden flight on 11 August 1952 and the following month appeared on static display at the 1952 SBAC Exhibition at Farnborough.

Towards the end of 1952 the more advanced Rolls Royce Avon-powered Comet 2 had begun to replace the Comet 1 and 1A on the production line, initially with BOAC's order for twelve aircraft and it was soon followed by orders from overseas airlines. Developed for transatlantic operation, the Comet 2 was 3ft longer and had its fuel capacity increased to 7,000 gallons. Trials showed that although it had a sufficient range for the South Atlantic it was still inadequate for non-stop operation over the North Atlantic. With the increasing interest in the Comet being shown by the world's airlines de Havilland expanded production. A production line was set-up by Short Bros. & Harland at their factory in Belfast and production started at de Havilland's Broughton factory, near Chester, an aircraft production factory that they had taken over from Vickers Armstrong in 1948. De Havilland started to build the prototype of the Comet 3, a stretched version of the Comet 2 powered by 10,000lb thrust Avon 502 engines. It was fitted with large pinion tanks fitted to the leading edge of the wing and its length was increased by 15ft to provide for a maximum of seventy-eight passengers.

The Comet's entry into service had been virtually trouble free, but on 26 October 1952 G-ALYZ (c/n06012) of BOAC, under the command of Captain H. Foot was written off in a take-off accident at Ciampino Airport, Rome. At 112 knots Captain Foot had lifted the aircraft off the runway, but almost immediately it had began to lose speed and the port wing dropped as it stalled onto the end of the runway, careering across rough ground beyond the end of the runway, shedding its undercarriage and pieces of wing. Although the integral fuel tanks in the wing had been ruptured and G-ALYZ came to rest in a pool of aviation fuel, there was no fire and all the thirty-five passengers and crew escaped from the wreckage uninjured. The investigation into the accident revealed that the tail of the Comet had scraped along the runway for the last 650 yards of the take-off run, confirming that the nose was too high and the wing partially stalled. It was realized that in that attitude the drag generated by the aircraft would be very high and would explain the reduction of speed noted by Captain Foot shortly before the crash. As nothing wrong was found with the aircraft the cause of the crash was put down to pilot error, as the captain had deviated from the take-off procedure by raising the nose too high before take-off speed had been achieved. BOAC transferred Captain Foot from the Comet fleet to freight operations on the Far East routes.

In March 1953 CPA's first Comet 1A CF-CUN, flown by their training pilot Captain Charles Pentland, left Hatfield on its delivery flight to Sydney, where it was to inaugurate CPA's service to Honolulu. Unfortunately, CF-CUN crashed on take-off from Karachi on 13 March in an accident virtually identical to that which befell G-ALYZ a few months before, only this time it burst into flames and the eleven crew and technicians aboard were killed. Again the accident was blamed on pilot error, but it was also realized that this was an error that was too easy to make. A third take-off accident occurred, when the UAT Comet F-BGSC (O6019) ran off the runway at Dakar on 25 June 1953 and was written-off. The de Havilland design team came to the conclusion that a wing that they had been developing for later versions of the Comet, that was to be operated at much higher weights, would solve the problem. This change saw the

The first Canadian Pacific Airline's Comet 1A CF-CUM, named Empress of Vancouver *on a flight from Hatfield on 15 August 1952. Following the crash of CF-CUN, their second aircraft, at Karachi on its delivery flight, CF-CUM was sold to BOAC and re-registered G-ANAV.*

introduction of a drooped leading edge on later Comets, which generated more lift on take-off and allowed the aircraft to climb away, even with the tail held down on the runway. In the meantime, the landing and take-off speeds of existing Comets was increased. Following the accident CPA sold their second Comet CF-CUM, before it entered service, to BOAC as G-ANAV to replace G-ALYZ.

Then on 2 May 1953, precisely a year after the Comet's first scheduled service, BOAC Comet G-ALYV (c/n06008), under the command of Captain Haddon, crashed shortly after take-off from Calcutta, *en route* for Delhi, killing all forty-three passengers and crew on board. The wreckage of G-ALYV, scattered over a large area, was located by an air search the following morning. It was evident that the aircraft had flown into a severe storm and had suffered complete structural failure in the turbulence. Unfortunately, the early Comets were not equipped with weather radar, which should have given them sufficient warning to have avoided the worst of the storms. However, after this accident, weather radar was to become standard fit on all Comets. A detailed investigation by the MOS experts at the Royal Aircraft Establishment at Farnborough of the wreckage of G-ALYV confirmed that the accident was due to severe external forces and not to any fault of the Comet airframe.

Tragically, worse was yet to come when, on 10 January 1954, the first production Comet 1 G-ALYP, under the command of Captain A. Gibson DFC, disintegrated and fell into the Mediterranean Sea near Elba, shortly after taking off from Rome, with the loss of the thirty-five passengers and crew. Within two days BOAC and Air France had grounded their Comet fleets, so that a detailed inspection could be carried out. In the meantime the Royal Navy, using its latest underwater detection gear, was commissioned to recover as much of the wreckage of G-ALYP from the sea bed as possible, a massive task as it was in 400ft of water and scattered over a large area. Despite this, the Royal Navy recovered a surprising amount of the wreckage for use in the investigation at RAE Farnborough. The inspections being carried out by BOAC and Air France and supported by technicians from de Havilland, failed to identify any problems that could have led to the loss of G-ALYP, so on 23 March 1954 the Comets were returned to passenger service, a decision that was to have tragic consequences.

Only two weeks after the Comets had returned to service another BOAC Comet, G-ALYY, on charter to South African Airways(SAA), commanded by SAA Captain W. Mostert, carrying twenty-one passengers and crew, took off from Rome on 8 April and disappeared over the Bay of Naples in similar circumstances to G-ALYP. Bodies and wreckage were picked up from the sea by HMS *Eagle*, which happened to be in the vicinity at the time. However, because the sea in the area was considered too deep and dangerous, it was not practical to recover the wreckage from the sea bed. BOAC immediately grounded their Comet fleet and later in the day their Certificates of Airworthiness were withdrawn, grounding all the Comets then in commercial operation. This was a devastating blow to de Havilland, the airlines and Britain. The minister responsible for aviation announced in parliament that the investigation into the accidents would be carried out as a major national research programme.

Comets that were *en route* when the grounding order was issued were subsequently flown back to base, in the case of BOAC London Airport, by volunteer crews flying in short stages and at low weight and restricted to under 20,000ft. Two Comets were allocated to DH at Hatfield and three were handed over to the RAE at Farnborough, joining the prototype G-ALVG which was already being used by them for research into the effect of fatigue on airframes. The investigating team at the RAE, under the leadership of Arnold Hall (later to become Sir Arnold), quickly started work on the investigation.

It was considered that one of the possible causes of the accidents was due to the pilots mishandling the controls and unintentionally over stressing the airframe or that the same result was caused by the powered flying controls losing control. To check the behaviour of a Comet at high altitude and high speed Comets, usually G-ANAV, were flown without cabin pressure by crews on oxygen. The aircraft carried out manoeuvres which generated loads on the airframe that were very close to the limit of the strength of the aircraft, well in excess of what would normally be applied in commercial service. During these test flights the Comet was always escorted and monitored by an English Electric Canberra.

At the RAE a large steel tank was built around the fuselage of G-ALYU (C/N 06007) which allowed the fuselage to be submerged under water. This massive structure, holding 250,000 gallons was built in six weeks and allowed the water pressure in the cabin to be raised and lowered to simulate the changes in pressure during the climb, cruise and descent of normal service flights. At the same time hydraulic rams attached to the wings, protruding out through the sides of the tank, applied loads to simulate the flexing of the wings in flight. On 24 June, after some six weeks of testing, the equivalent of 9,000 flying hours, the fuselage failed from fatigue. This was an incredibly short fatigue life, when compared with what the company had previously estimated, using data from tests on sections of fuselage obtained earlier in the Comet programme.

In parallel with the water tank test the wreckage of G-ALYP, that was being progressively recovered from the seabed by the Royal Navy, the pieces of fuselage were assembled to a wooden framework, so that each section would be positioned in its original location. The team involved with the investigation of the wreckage was led by Eric Ripley. They inspected all the wreckage in great detail as it arrived at Farnborough and soon came to the conclusion that the pressure cabin had failed in an explosive decompression, with the initial cracks developing in the forward cabin roof. This related closely to the results of the water tank test, but it was not until August when the appropriate section of fuselage structure had been recovered from the sea, that there was indisputable proof that the Comets broke up because of fatigue failure of the forward cabin roof skins, starting at the rear automatic direction

The seventh production Comet 1, G-ALYU, in the water tank at RAE Farnborough in 1954. The aircraft had completed 1,230 flights when it was withdrawn from service and installed in the tank. The fuselage failed after a further 1,830 simulated flights. The tests provided evidence for the Court of Inquiry into the accidents to G-ALYP and G-ALYY.

finder (ADF) panel. At this point, Arnold Hall and his team had brought the largest and most comprehensive air accident investigation to a satisfactory conclusion. All that was left was the preparation of a detailed report, which was to run to some 380 pages and was the main document in the Court of Inquiry that was held at Church Hall, Westminster. The court's conclusion was that no-one was to blame as de Havillands had designed and built the Comet to accepted well-established aeronautical engineering principles. Following the investigation, many techniques were changed and those proposed by de Havilland to correct the Comet's weaknesses were approved by the court.

At the time of the accidents Comet 2s were on the verge of entering service with BOAC, and their first Comet 2 G-AMXA which had made its first flight on 27 August 1953 was displayed at the SBAC show at Farnborough in September. However, they were included in the grounding order and at the same time Comet production was halted, although assembly of the prototype Comet 3 G-ANLO was continued at Hatfield. The maiden flight of G-ANLO took place on 19 July 1954 at Hatfield, in the hands of John Cunningham and Peter Bugge and made a dramatic appearance at the Farnborough Air Display in September, coinciding with the Court of Inquiry.

It was decided that it would not be economical to modify the surviving Comet 1s for a return to commercial passenger service, but the two RCAF Comet 1As were rebuilt at de Havilland's Broughton factory. The major changes that were introduced were new, thicker gauge fuselage skins, round windows to replace the original rectangular apertures while the engine jet pipes were swept outboard to keep the jet effluxes away from the fuselage, so reducing the buffeting of the fuselage skins. These modified aircraft were returned to the RCAF as Comet 1XBs in 1957 and were to provide many years useful service. Similarly, two of the Air France Comet 1As were also modified at Broughton for the MOS, that used them for research purposes.

It was realized that there would be a significant increase in the weight of the modified Comet 2, which would make it unsuitable for BOAC's planned use on its South American routes, so de Havilland decided that it would concentrate its sales efforts on the Comet 3 and subsequent developments to the airlines. Only eighteen Comet 2s were built, including Comet 2X G-ALYT and two for structural testing. A number had been completed and others were already on the production line, but all required extensive modification to meet the latest requirements. Following the decision to build only a small number of Comet 2s, production at Short Bros. & Harland, which like all other Comet production had been postponed at the time of the accidents, was cancelled and the partly-completed Comets were transported to Broughton in 1955. Although thirteen of the Comet 2s were allotted to the MOS and the RAF and the two civil ones were only to be used for development flying, it was decided that, as a precaution, the Comet 2 should obtain a full commercial Certificate of Airworthiness (C of A) in addition to the normal approval for British military aircraft, Controller Aircraft (CA) release. To meet the stringent new regulations two Comet 2 airframes (C/Ns 06036 and 06038), incorporating all the fatigue remedial modifications, were used for static strength and fatigue tests. The full scale fatigue tests carried out in the new water tank at Hatfield confirmed the aircraft to have a safe life well in excess of the RAF requirement and, in May 1956, the Comet 2 was granted an unrestricted C of A. All of the Comet 2s were built at Hatfield and completed during 1956-1957 with the exception of the last, XK716 (c/n 06045), which was the first Comet built at Broughton and flew for the first time on 6 May 1957, on its delivery flight to Hatfield.

Ten Comet 2s were allotted to the RAF's Transport Command for use by No.216 Squadron. The first to be delivered to 216 Squadron at RAF Lyneham on 7 July 1956 was XK670, a crew trainer designated a Comet T.2. This was followed shortly afterwards by another T.2 XK669, which enabled the squadron to gain experience of the type before the arrival of the eight transport Comet C.2s, which fitted out for forty-four passengers, were used for normal transport duties.

Operational flying with the Comets started on 23 June 1956 when Comet T.2 XM670 flew the Air Minister to Moscow for the Soviet Air Force Day celebrations. Later in the year the Comets were in regular use, flying to Malta and Cyprus in support of Operation Musketeer, the Suez Crisis. Regular flights were provided to support the missile range at Woomera, in South Australia and the nuclear bombing tests at Christmas Island. Towards the end of 1959 all of 216 Squadron's Comets were allocated names, XK669 *Taurus*, XK670 *Corvus*, XK671 *Aquila*, XK695 *Perseus*, XK696 *Orion*, XK697 *Cygnus*, XK698 *Pegasus*, XK699 *Sagittarius*, XK715 *Columba* and XK716 *Cepheus*. The Squadron continued to operate the Comet C.2s until their withdrawal from service in March 1967.

Three other Comet 2s, XK655, XK659 and XK663, were modified by Marshall of Cambridge and fitted with special equipment for electronic intelligence surveillance by the RAF's No.90 Signals Group, becoming Comet C.2Rs. These Comets were issued to No.192 Squadron at RAF Watton in August 1958, just as it was renumbered No.51 Squadron. They continued to operate alongside the Squadron's Canberras until they were withdrawn from service in November 1974.

Two Comet 2Es G-AMXD and G-AMXK, fitted with Avon524s in the outboard nacelles and Avon 504s in the inner, were used for route proving trials as part of the Comet 4 development programme. G-AMXD subsequently went to the RAE as XN453 and was used for long range radio trials, until they were withdrawn from use in 1973 and scrapped in 1974; while G-AMXK was used by Smith's Industries at Hatfield for autopilot trials, before going to the Blind Landing Experimental Unit (BLEU) at RAE Bedford as XV144 in November 1966. It was withdrawn from use in 1971 and scrapped in 1975.

BOAC had ordered five Comet 3s in 1954, but had later cancelled them with the intention

The first Comet 2, G-AMXA, in the BOAC colour scheme, taking-off from Hatfield. It was not delivered to BOAC and was subsequently modified to Comet C2R standard and delivered to 192 Squadron.

of reviewing the situation when the accident investigation at Farnborough had been completed. However, development of the Comet 3 continued at Hatfield and, during 1955, de Havilland proposed the Comet 4, powered by 10,500lb thrust Avon 524 engines and increased fuel capacity, giving it the capability to operate on the North Atlantic routes.

The prototype Comet 3 G-ANLO continued its flight test programme and on 2 December 1955 with John Cunningham and Peter Bugge at the controls it left Hatfield on a round-the- world flight, via Australia, arriving back on 28 December. The flight was the first encirclement of the globe and included the first trans-pacific flight by a jet airliner. Later G-ANLO was modified to take the larger Avon 523s and so be more representative of the Comet 4, flying for the first time with these engines on 25 February 1957. G-ANLO, with the two Comet 2Es G-AMXD and G-AMXK, were used throughout 1957 for route proving trials. Rolls Royce noise suppressors were later fitted to G-ANLO for trials and these became standard for all the production Comet 4s. In the spring of 1958 thrust reversers were fitted to the outboard engines of G-ANLO for landing tests and, although successful, it was too late to introduce them on the early production Series 4 aircraft.

Capital Airlines in the USA placed an order in July 1956 for four Comet 4s and ten Comet 4As, which were designed specifically for the airline's short and medium length routes. The 4A was to have a wingspan reduced by 7ft and the fuselage lengthened by 40in, enabling it to accommodate up to ninety-two tourist class passengers. Unfortunately, Capital Airlines ran into financial difficulties and the order was cancelled. However, at about the same time British European Airways Corporation (BEA) started to take an interest in a short-to-medium range Comet. Like the 4A, this Comet, identified as the Series 4B, had its wingspan reduced by 7ft to increase the cruising speed at lower altitude, but the fuselage length was increased by 78in to accommodate a maximum of 102 passengers and the pinion tanks were deleted. As part of the 4B development programme, the Comet 3 G-ANLO had its pinion tanks removed and span reduced to be aerodynamically representative. In this guise it became known as the Comet 3B and acting in effect as the prototype Comet 4B, started its test flight programme on 21 August 1958. G-ANLO, as XP915, was delivered to the Blind Landing Experimental Unit (BLEU) at RAE Bedford on 21 June 1961. However, on 19 January 1971 it was involved in a potentially serious incident when it was cleared to hold on the centre-line and threshold of the runway at Bedford. While holding, the aircraft was struck on the fin and rudder by the fully deployed flap of the first production DH Trident 3B G-AWZA which was carrying out a low overshoot. Much of the fin and rudder of XP915 was removed and the flap and undersurface of the port wing of the Trident was damaged. XP915 was repaired and returned to service, but was placed in storage in 1972. It was later used by the RAE for tests into the effectiveness of using urea formaldehyde for runway braking.

BOAC maintained its enthusiasm for the Comet, particularly as the Series 4 was able to fly the North Atlantic, albeit with a stop at Gander on the westbound flight to take on more fuel. The eastbound flight, assisted by the jetstream would make it possible to fly non-stop between New York and London. In 1957 BOAC ordered nineteen Comet 4s (G-APDA to G-APDT) that were intended for their services to Africa and the Far East. The first of these, G-APDA, flew for the first time at Hatfield with the usual Cunningham and Bugge team at the controls on 27 April 1958. After completing its development flight test programme, G-APDA joined the two Comet 2Es for the final phase of the certification trials. Flown by John Cunningham on 14 September, G-APDA flew the 7,925 miles from Hong Kong to London in just over sixteen hours. Three days later it flew to Gander, Newfoundland in the record time of five hours forty-seven minutes at the start of a series of flights that ended in Buenos Aires, calling at Montreal, Vancouver, Mexico City and Lima *en route*.

Unfortunately, during the long delay caused by the investigation and the major re-design of the Comet, de Havilland lost the significant lead that it had in the design and manufacture of jet transports. The Tupolev Tu-104 entered airline service in the USSR in 1956 and the Boeing 707, which was due to enter service with Pan American World Airways (Pan Am) in October 1958. The Comet 4 received its Certificate of Airworthiness from the Air Registration Board on 29 September 1958, just six days after the American Federal Aviation Authority had issued the certificate for the Boeing 707. Primarily, for public relations purposes, as neither the Comet 4 nor the early Boeing 707 had the range to operate across the North Atlantic non-stop, an unofficial race to be the first to inaugurate the first pure jet service across the Atlantic began. Pan Am announced that they would launch a daily service between New York and Paris on 26 October. However, BOAC was the winner when, on 4 October 1958, Comet 4s made simultaneous east and westbound crossings of the Atlantic, carrying paying passengers. G-APDC, commanded by Captain R.E. Millichap, flew from London to New York, via Gander, in ten hours twenty-two minutes and G-APDB, commanded by Captain T.B. Stoney, flew non-stop from New York to London in six hours eleven minutes. Initially, the trans-Atlantic service was weekly, but from 13 November it was increased to a daily service. On 19 December a weekly Comet London to Montreal service was also introduced. During 1959 Comet 4s were introduced on the Johannesburg, Ceylon, Australia and Tokyo routes. The BOAC Comets were withdrawn from the north Atlantic services in October 1960 with the arrival of the intercontinental Rolls Royce Conway powered Boeing 707-420. This released more Comets for additional Canadian services and the opening of routes to the Caribbean, Chile and Iran.

The first export order for the Comet 4 was from Aerolineas Argentinas that placed an order for six. LV-PLM (c/n 06408) the first of these, making its maiden flight on 11 December 1958, was delivered on 2 March 1959 and was followed shortly afterwards by LV-PLO and LV-PLP. The remaining three, LV-POY, LV-POZ and LV-PPA, were delivered to Argentina during 1960. Aerolineas Argentinas inaugurated its first Comet service from Buenos Aires to Santiago, Chile on 16 April 1959, with services to Europe and the USA starting the following month. The only other order for the Comet 4 was from East African Airways who ordered two, VP-KPJ

The prototype Comet 3 G-ANLO during its first flight on 19 July 1954, showing its lengthened fuselage and wing pinion tanks. Power was provided by four 10,000lb thrust Rolls-Royce Avon RA26 Mk502 engines. Although successful in winning a number of orders, de Havilland decided not to put the type into production and G-ANLO was used for the development of its successor the Comet 4.

and VP-KPK, both being delivered to Nairobi in July 1960.

G-APMA (c/n 06421), the first of fourteen of the short-haul Comet 4Bs ordered by BEA, flew for the first time on 27 June 1959. It was initially retained by de Havilland for certification trials, before being delivered early in 1960. Scheduled services started on 1 April 1960 with four aircraft, G-APMA to Nice, G-APMF to Moscow, G-APMD to Tel Aviv while G-APMB flew from Tel Aviv to London. Four Comet 4Bs were also supplied to Olympic Airways, who operated them in a consortium with BEA.

The next development, the Comet 4C, was an intermediate range version, using in effect the longer, higher capacity fuselage of the 4B, but with the long span wing of the 4, with its higher fuel capacity. Impressed by the Comet 4's ability to operate from high airfields in hot climates Compania Mexicana de Aviacion de CV (Mexicana), the national airline of Mexico, placed an order for three Comet 4Cs. The first Comet 4C in the Mexicana colour scheme, but bearing the British registration G-AOVU, flew at Hatfield on 31 October 1959 with W.P.I. Fillingham at the controls. Although G-AOVU was retained at Hatfield until it was delivered to Mexico as XA-NAR in June 1960, the second Mexicana Comet was delivered in January and entered service shortly afterwards. The emergence of the new Comet aroused interest among other airlines. Misrair, later United Arab Airlines (UAA), ordered a total of nine, Middle East Airlines four, Sudan Airways two, Aerolineas Argentinas one, Kuwait Airways two, and East African Airways one. The government of Saudi Arabia ordered one SA-R-7 (c/n 06461), which was luxuriously furnished for the personal use of King Ibn Saud. It was delivered on 15 June 1962 but unfortunately it crashed, killing all the crew, in the Italian Alps on 20 March 1963.

Five Comet 4Cs, XR395 to XR399, were built at Broughton for the RAF's Transport Command as Comet C.Mk.4s and were delivered to No.216 Squadron at Lyneham between January and April 1962. The Comet C.4s were normally equipped to carry ninety-four rearward-facing passengers, but role equipment was available for conversion to an air ambulance or VIP transport. In its ambulance role it could carry twelve stretchers, forty-seven sitting cases and six attendants. For the next five years 216 Squadron operated the new Comets alongside their existing Comet C.2s until the last one was withdrawn from service in March 1967. The Comet C.4s continued to operate all over the world until the Squadron was disbanded on 30 June 1975 as part of a package of government defence cuts. The five Comet C.4s were flown to RAF Leconfield to await disposal.

Comet production finished in 1962, although some of those stored on the assembly tracks were completed later. One Comet, 4C XS235 (c/n 06473), built at Broughton and fitted out at Hatfield as a radio trials laboratory aircraft, was delivered to the Navigation and Radio Division of the A&AEE at Boscombe Down on 2 December 1963. Two were completed for Kuwait Airways, the last being delivered on 27 January 1964 and the last civil Comet was SU-ANI (06475) which was delivered to United Arab Airlines on 26 February 1964, leaving just two airframes (c/ns 06476 and 06477) unsold on the track at Broughton.

With the arrival of later versions of the Boeing 707s and the new VC10s, larger and more economical jet airliners that were more suited to BOAC's routes, the Comets were withdrawn from service. BOAC's last scheduled Comet service was flown by G-APDM from Auckland to London on 11 November 1965. In their seven years of service only one had been lost, and that was when G-APDH crash-landed because of undercarriage problems at Singapore Airport on 22 March 1964. Six of the BOAC Comets were acquired in 1965 by Malaysian Airways, which the following year became Malaysian-Singapore Airlines. Although, initially, all the Comets were registered in Malaysia, three were later given Singapore registrations. The remaining twelve of the surviving BOAC Comet fleet were subsequently disposed of: four went to Dan-Air, two to Mexicana, one to East African Airways, one to Aerovias Ecuatorianas (AREA), one to Middle East Airlines, one to Kuwait Airways and the last two to the Ministry of Technology for use as flying test beds.

The Comet 4Bs continued in service with BEA and Olympic Airways until G-APMA, the first Comet 4B flew BEA's last scheduled Comet service on 31 October 1971. However, seven of BEA's Comet 4Bs continued to operate in virtually the same colour scheme, as they were transferred to BEA Airtours, a subsidiary company set up by BEA to provide inclusive tour flights for various package tour operators. Channel Airways based at Stansted Airport bought five Comet 4Bs from BEA, although four of these were aircraft that had been operated by Olympic Airways and returned to BEA only a short time before they were delivered to Channel Airways.

Dan-Air had started in the early 1950s as the aircraft brokering division of Davies and Newman Ltd, a long established shipbrokers. Initially, it had concentrated on freighting, but had subsequently progressed primarily into inclusive tour and charter work, but also operated a few scheduled services. The company had seen that the future of their business lay with jet powered aircraft and when BOAC's Comet 4s came onto the market Dan-Air took the opportunity to acquire two in 1966. The Comet 4 was not ideal for Dan-Air's style of operation and so their aircraft were modified to increase the passenger capacity to ninety-nine. The success of their first two Comets led to further acquisitions from BOAC, a third in 1967 and a fourth in 1968. During the next three years Dan-Air expanded its Comet fleet by fifteen, buying up Comets as they came on to the market. These included their first Comet 4Cs, two from Kuwait Airways and one from Aerolineas Argentinas. Although Dan-Air had the seating capacity of their Comet 4s further increased from ninety-nine to 106, it could still not match the 119 passengers that could be accommodated in the longer fuselage of the 4C.

The first Comet 4, G-APDA, made its maiden flight on 27 April 1958 and was retained by de Havilland for development until delivered to BOAC on 24 February 1959.

When, early in 1972 BEA Airtours started to replace its Comet 4Bs with Boeing 707s, Dan-Air acquired two of these short haul Comets, which were the ideal for Dan-Air's operation. Later in the year a further five 4Bs were bought from Channel Airways, but only four were delivered, as one was broken-up at Southend to provide spares for the expanding Dan-Air fleet. The year 1973 saw the delivery of a further eight 4Bs from BEA Airtours and a 4C from Middle East Airlines. When defence cuts in 1975 resulted in the disbandment of the RAF's No.216 Squadron, their five Comet C.4s and remaining spares were sold to Dan-Air. Two Comet 4Cs were acquired from Sudan Airways and, finally, in October 1976 four 4Cs were bought from Egyptair. Of these only one of the ex-Sudan Airways aircraft entered service, as all the rest were broken up for spares. Dan-Air started to withdraw the Comet from service in 1980. The last commercial flight by a Comet was made by G-BDIW, an ex-RAF aircraft, on 9 November 1980. By this time forty-nine Comets had passed through Dan-Air's hands, well over half of the seventy-seven Comet 4 variants that were built, including the fatigue test airframe.

However, this was not the end of the Comet, because in 1980 there were still three Comets, and the Nimrod prototype XV147 that had originally been built as a Comet, flying at the MOD research establishments. XW626(c/n.06419), ex-G-APDS of BOAC, was in use for trials with the Nimrod AEW radar and, after completion of the trials on 28 August 1981, the aircraft was relegated to apprentice training before being scrapped with the closure of the RAE Thurleigh Airfield in April 1994. Another ex-BOAC Comet 4 G-APDF had been delivered to RAE Farnborough as XV814 on 7 October 1968 and was subsequently fitted with a large pannier under the nose and a large Nimrod-type dorsal fin. After delivery to Boscombe Down on 28 January 1993, it was used as a source of spares for the remaining Comet XS235 and was scrapped on 12 August 1997.

The last airworthy Comet 4C XS235 (c/n06473) spent thirty-four years as a trials aircraft with the Navigation and Radio Division of the A&AEE and later its successor DERA at Boscombe Down. It was originally intended that it would be withdrawn from service in 1995, but it survived until 1997, making its last operational flight on 14 March. When XS235 was offered for sale de Havilland Aircraft Heritage Museum bought it with the intention of preserving it at Hatfield. However, there was a change of plan and it was flown to British Aviation Heritage at Bruntingthorpe Airfield, where it gives occasional demonstrations of fast taxiing. It is however, the hope of many that XS235 will ultimately be returned to flying status and an example of the most beautiful airliner ever built will take to the air again.

The Chester-built Comet 4C, XS235 Canopus, on its arrival at Bruntingthorpe on 30 October 1997 at the end of what is likely to have been its last flight, for preservation by British Aviation Heritage. Until then Canopus had spent all its thirty-four year operational life as a flying laboratory with the Navigation and Radio Division of the A&AEE (later DERA).

HS801 Nimrod

Towards the end of the 1950s it had become obvious that the Avro Shackleton was obsolescent and would need replacing during the next decade. With this in mind the Air Ministry issued Operational Requirement No.OR350 and immediately both Vickers Armstrong, which was soon to become part of the British Aircraft Corporation (BAC), and the Avro Division of Hawker Siddeley Aviation (HSA) started to prepare design studies for a Shackleton replacement.

Vickers Armstrong, at Weybridge, prepared projects based on their existing civil airliners, the VC10, Vanguard and sometime later the BAC 111. One of these projects was a very impressive variable geometry version of the VC10. Initially, Avro's projects were totally new designs, presumably because their only contemporary civil airliner, the Avro 748, was too small to be modified into a maritime reconnaissance aircraft to meet OR350. Avro's first project, the AVRO 775 was a three-engined aircraft powered by two wing-mounted Rolls-Royce Tyne propeller turbine engines and one Rolls-Royce RB168 high by-pass jet engine mounted in the

The last Comet 4C on the track at the Hawker Siddeley factory at Broughton, Chester, in the process of being converted into the first prototype Nimrod XV148. The new radar nose and skirts for the weapons bay are being fitted and the new, deeper wing centre section with the larger air intakes for the Rolls-Royce Spey engines can be clearly seen.

tail. Discussions with representatives of both the Air Ministry and the RAF's Coastal Command led Avro to believe that a slightly more advanced project than the Avro 775 was required, because it was considered that the Avro 775 had insufficient transit speed and space available for the carriage of stores. Some eight months later, in November 1961, the brochure on the second project, the Avro 776, was issued. It was powered by three tail-mounted Rolls-Royce RB178 Super Conway turbo-fan engines. During the design of the Avro 776 it was realized that the fuselage size was similar to that of the de Havilland Trident and so every effort was made to have it identical to the Trident, although modification was necessary for the carriage of military stores. Avro's third and final original design to OR350 was the Avro 784, which also proved to be the last project to appear under the Avro name. The Avro 784 was a conventional aircraft powered by four wing-mounted, propeller turbine engines, which met all the requirements, except for transit speed.

The Advanced Project Group (APG) of HSA, based at Kingston-upon-Thames, also produced two project studies, HSA1010A a turbo-prop aircraft and the HSA1011F a very advanced variable geometry design powered by four rear-mounted jet engines.

In the middle of 1963 Air Staff Target (AST) 357 was issued by the Air Ministry. This was essentially similar to AST.350 but was more precisely defined and in some respects it represented a more severe requirement, particularly in relation to operational systems. In August 1963 the Avro Whitworth Division, as it had become, following the merger of the Avro and Whitworth Gloster Divisions of HSA, received a request from the Ministry of Aviation (MOA) for Feasibility Studies based on AST.357.

The Avro Whitworth Feasibility Study was submitted to the MOA in October 1963 and included not only the Avro 776 and 784, but also two derivatives of the DH Trident, identified as the Trident MR1 and MR2 and two Maritime Reconnaissance versions of the projected AW 681military transport aircraft. The Trident MR1 was a basic civil Trident 1E with a pannier fitted beneath the fuselage to carry the military stores, new, larger outer wings that would carry additional fuel and wing-mounted external tanks. The Trident MR2 was similar to the MR1 but it was fitted with a totally new wing, similar to that proposed for the Avro 776. In parallel with the design of the new aircraft companies in the avionics industry werer designing a new operational system to meet AST 357. However, by the end of 1963, it was becoming evident that the system would not be available before 1972. It must be assumed that BAC had carried out a similar feasibility study based on their VC10, Vanguard and BAC111 aircraft. Their was some fear in the Avro camp that BAC might have the advantage with the large size of the VC10 offering much greater development potential.

However, in February 1964, with the rising costs and time-scale slippages of the Shackleton Modernization Programme, the MOA undertook a re-assessment of the whole situation. The conclusion was that the Shackleton should be phased out of service in 1968 but, as the AST 357 operational system would not be available, an interim aircraft should enter service with the operational capability of the Shackleton. It should, however, have sufficient development potential to allow for the introduction of the more advanced operational system when it became available. This change of timescale excluded any possibility of a totally new design being selected, but it was always unlikely because of the very high cost of developing a new design. Following discussions between Avro Whitworth and the MOA the most likely projects appeared to be a Trident 1E, fitted with a weapons pannier and wing-mounted, external fuel tanks or the slightly more advanced Trident MR1. Ranged against these proposals were the maritime VC10, Vanguard and the BAC 1011, a maritime version of the BAC 111. Also under consideration were the Lockheed Orion and the Breguet Atlantique. The RAF at this time had a marked preference for pure jet-powered aircraft which would have gone against the selection of the Vanguard, Orion and Atlantique. For reasons of safety, the RAF had a preference for four-engined aircraft in the maritime reconnaissance role, which always seemed sensible when spending long periods patrolling over the sea, and this would also have gone against the twin-engined Atlantique.

De Havilland had also been working on a maritime version of the DH106 Comet. Sometime in the middle of 1964 it had gained favour with the MOA and at about the same time responsibility for the project passed to the Avro Whitworth division of HSA. It is believed that the addition of the Comet to the list of projects was partly due to the RAF's preference for four-engined aircraft and with the increasing urgency for a Shackleton replacement the Comet was virtually ideal, with all the jigs and tools still available and the last two Comet 4Cs still unsold on the track at Broughton. The design departments of Avro Whitworth, supported by the de Havilland division, prepared a type specification for the HS801 Comet Maritime Reconnaissance Aircraft which was issued in December 1964 and in February 1965 it was announced that a Maritime Comet was to be ordered to replace the sixty Shackleton Mk 2s that remained in service with the RAF. At the time it was intended that the Shackleton Mk3s would be upgraded to phase III standard, which included the introduction of Bristol Siddeley Viper boost engines in the rear of the outer engine nacelles and would continue to operate alongside the HS801 until 1978. However, by the end of 1972 the Shackleton MR 3 was at the end of its fatigue life and would require the wings to be re-sparred if they were to remain in service. This also coincided with the British government's withdrawal from its worldwide defence role so the Shackletons were withdrawn from service.

Air Staff Requirement (ASR) 381, the final specification for the Shackleton replacement, was issued on 4 June 1964 and this defined the role for the aircraft as:

1. To detect, fix and destroy surfaced and submerged submarines, both conventional and nuclear;
2. To detect and shadow enemy surface units and forces;
3. To conduct wide area surveillance;
4. To make limited air to surface strikes against individual vessels;
5. To perform search and rescue;
6. To undertake an emergency trooping role.

The proposed HS801 Comet maritime reconnaissance aircraft was basically a Comet 4C reduced in length, by the removal of the 78in plug forward of the wing, to the length of the Comet 4. The wing centre section was also modified to house the Rolls-Royce Spey turbofan engines that were being introduced, because of their much better specific fuel consumption than that offered by the existing Avons. Weapons were to be carried in an unpressurized, ventral pannier running almost the entire length of the fuselage and blending into a fairing at the nose which housed the scanner for the ASV21 radar. It is this pannier that is the most distinctive feature of the HS801, resulting in the biggest change to the Comet shape. To compensate for the extra side area of the pannier a dorsal fin was introduced and the Electronic Counter Measures (ECM) was located in a fairing on top of the fin. A tail boom was introduced for the Magnetic Anomaly Detector (MAD) which had to be kept as far away as possible from the metallic mass of the aircraft. A 70-million candlepower searchlight was mounted in the nose of the starboard pinion tank and could be directed by the co-pilot and two wing strong points were introduced to carry pylon mounted air-to-surface missiles. Although the four windscreen panels remained the same as the original Comet, the direct vision and side windows were deepened and eyebrow windows were added over the side windows to assist the pilots in tight turns at low level over the sea.

An Instruction to Proceed (ITP) with the HS801 was issued to Hawker Siddeley in May 1965 and this was followed by a contract in January 1966. This £95 million fixed price contract was one of the largest ever placed with a British aircraft manufacturer. The requirement was for thirty-eight production aircraft to specification MR.254D & P and the conversion of the two remaining Comet 4Cs that were still being stored on the production line at Broughton into prototypes for the development programme. Hawker Siddeley Aviation were in effect the prime contractor, responsible for the management of the development and production of the HS801 as a complete weapons system, which required a significant expansion of their avionics department.

XV147, the second Nimrod prototype, was converted from the penultimate Comet 4C at Woodford, but was not fully representative of the Nimrod as it retained its original Rolls-Royce Avon engines. XV147 flew for the first time as a Nimrod on 31 July 1967 and is shown here at Woodford a few days later with a Shackleton MR3 in the background.

The penultimate Comet (c/n 06476), which was structurally complete was prepared to a one flight standard, with the serial number XV147, and was flown from Broughton to Woodford by John Cunningham on 25 October 1965. This aircraft was modified at Woodford so that externally it appeared to be to HS801 standard but retained Avon engines and, as it was to be used for the flight testing of the HS801 systems, initially the Nav/Tac system, the electrical generators were changed to provide the additional power. At the same time it was decided that, as the last Comet (c/n 06477) on the track at Broughton had not been completed, it would be more conducive to convert it to full HS801 aerodynamic standard, particularly in regard to the changes necessary to the wing centre section to accommodate Spey engines. Changes were also made to the electrical, fuel and hydraulic systems. This aircraft, after conversion at Broughton and with the serial number XV148, made its first flight from Broughton on 23 May 1967 with John Cunningham at the controls and J.G. (Jimmy) Harrison the Chief Test Pilot at HSA Woodford as co-pilot with a crew of five. After a flight of seventy-five minutes XV148 landed at Woodford where it was retained for handling and performance trials. Shortly into the flight test programme it was confirmed that there was a minor problem with directional stability which had first been encountered during wind tunnel testing. This problem was quickly resolved by the introduction of a much larger dorsal fin, which was fitted to XV148 in June 1967.

The HS801 could quite legitimately have become the Comet MR5, having initially been referred to as the Maritime Comet. However, in mid-1967 Lord Shackleton, the Minister of Defence and the RAF announced that the HS801 Maritime Comet had been given the name Nimrod, who was a biblical figure mentioned in chapter ten of the book of Genesis: 'Nimrod, became the first of the kings and was a mighty hunter, blessed of God'.

The second prototype XV147 flew for the first time as a Nimrod at Woodford on 31 July 1967, with Jimmy Harrison at the controls. For the first flight it was fitted with the original small dorsal fin but this was replaced by the new larger one before its second flight. After completing its flight test schedule XV147 was transferred to the RAE at Farnborough, where it was used for the development of the NAV/TAC system.

Production of Comet related sub-assemblies continued at the various HSA factories that had been built for the Comet programme. The jigs and tools in most cases had not been used since the end of Comet production and had to be refurbished and modified where necessary. The Chester factory remained responsible for the fuselage and centre section and subsequently the outer wings which were transferred there with the closure of the Portsmouth factory. Engine intakes and tailplanes were built at Hatfield and new assemblies, specific to Nimrod, were produced at Chadderton. All the sub-assemblies were delivered to Woodford for final assembly and flight testing.

The first new build Nimrod XV226 made its maiden flight at Woodford on 28 June 1968 with Jimmy Harrison at the controls. This and the next three production Nimrods XV227, XV228 and XV229 were retained by HSA for the flight development programme. XV148 and two production aircraft (XV227 and XV228) were used for evaluation trials at the A&AEE Boscombe Down during 1968 and 1969, with Controller Aircraft (CA) release being achieved in the autumn of 1969. Shortly afterwards, the RAF received its first Nimrod, when XV230 was delivered to the Maritime Operational Training Unit (MOTU) at St Mawgan, Cornwall on 2 October 1969. Training of the first RAF Nimrod crews started almost immediately. The following month, Coastal Command was disbanded and replaced by No.18

The roll-out of the first production Nimrod MR1, XV226, at Woodford on 23 May 1968. After use for development by Hawker Siddeley and the A&AEE, it was delivered to the RAF at Kinloss on 15 January 1973.

(Maritime) Group of Strike Command. To mark the change XV230 joined with nine Shackletons for the flypast ceremony. Then on 1 July 1970 MOTU was re-designated No.236 Operational Conversion Unit (OCU).

No.201 Squadron, based at Kinloss, was the first operational squadron to receive the Nimrod, with the first aircraft arriving in October 1970, by July 1971 it had received ten. Nos.120 and 206 Squadrons, also based at Kinloss, started to re-equip with Nimrods before the end of 1970. The fourth squadron to re-equip with Nimrods was No.42 at St Mawgan in April 1971, and finally in July 1971 No.203 at Luqa in Malta.

As production progressed at Woodford a contract was received by HSA for the design, development and production of three special HS801R Nimrod R.1s for the RAF's Electronic Reconnaissance support role, to replace the Comet C.2Rs, which were being operated by No.51 Squadron. Delivery of these aircraft, identified as XW664, XW665 and XW666, commenced in July 1971 and they operated alongside the Comets until the last of them was phased out in November 1974. The Nimrod R.1 had many significant differences to the standard Nimrod MR1, particularly in regard to the equipment fit required for the new role, but the most obvious difference was the deletion of the MAD boom and its replacement with a small radome. The crew required to operate the Nimrod R.1 was an increase on the eleven usually carried on the Nimrod MR1 and must have put some pressure on the limited space available in a Nimrod fuselage.

The Nimrod MR1 was only considered to be an interim aircraft, as the urgency to get it into service did not allow sufficient time to complete the development of the systems required to fully meet AST357. Consequently, before the production of the MR1s was complete HSA were already planning a communications refit to meet ASR828 and ASR863, to be followed by a much more extensive avionics refit to AST872. XV229 was selected as the development aircraft for the communications refit, with fixed fittings also being installed in XV147 which was designated the back-up aircraft for the development programme. The resulting modifications for the communications update were installed in the Nimrod fleet at the Nimrod Major Service Unit (NMSU) at Kinloss by a Contractors Working Party (CWP) provided by HSA.

During the preparations for the Nimrod entering service Strike Command considered that, whenever possible, they should retain control of all the aircraft in the fleet. As part of this policy it was decided that, rather than hand aircraft to a maintenance unit for major servicing a Nimrod Major Servicing Unit, manned by RAF personnel and under the direct control of 18 Group Strike Command would be set up at RAF Kinloss. This plan was approved because of the relatively small number of Nimrods and their considerable importance for the defence of the UK at that critical time in the cold war. Consequently, with just a few exceptions, all the major servicing of Nimrods to date have been carried out by the NMSU. However, in the mid-1990s major changes took place as part of the government policy of civilianizing non-front line activities of the services and the NMSU was put out to tender and was subsequently taken over by FRA/SERCO.

From the outset HSA was keen to gain export customers for the Nimrod, the prime targets being Australia and Canada, but also a number of smaller air forces: Japan, India, Argentina, Holland, Brazil, and South Africa. Australia looked a rather doubtful customer, having previously ordered ten Lockheed P3B Orions. However, when they considered a further batch full consideration was given to the Nimrod, the later P3C version of the Orion, the Breguet Atlantique and ASW versions of the Boeing 707 and Douglas DC10. Even though at the end the competition was reduced to just the Nimrod and Orion, it was really inevitable that it was the Orion that was ordered. Unfortunately, despite all the efforts made by HAS, supported by the British Government, they failed to win any of the overseas sales, generally losing out to Lockheed, leaving the RAF as the sole operator of the Nimrod. It is understood that the Orion had the advantage on price, but there also appeared to be a prejudice against the use of pure jet-powered aircraft for the long-range maritime patrol role.

The first Nimrod, R1 XW664, at Woodford in May 1971. It flew for the first time at Woodford on 22 March 1971 and was delivered to 51 Squadron at Wyton where the special avionics systems were installed.

An additional eight Nimrod MR1s, XZ280 to XZ287 were ordered in January 1972 and delivery of these commenced in April 1975. By this time design of the avionics refit for the Nimrod MR1 was underway and HSA was also considering the feasibility of using Nimrods for the Airborne Early Warning role as a replacement for the Shackleton AEW 2. These developments resulted in only five of the second batch being delivered as MR 1s, the other three were delivered as 'green' aircraft, with only a minimal equipment fit sufficient for a single delivery flight to Kinloss. There they were stored until they were returned to Woodford. One, XZ284, for the Avionic refit, made it, in effect, the only new build Nimrod MR2. The remaining two were held for conversion into Nimrod AEW 3s.

The avionics refit covered by Modification No.3,000 converted the Nimrod MR1 into the MR2 and saw a major upgrade of the radar, acoustics and the introduction of a central tactical system (CTS). The new EMI Searchwater radar replaced the obsolete ASV Mk.21, that had originally been used on the Shackleton. Searchwater was a state-of-the-art, computer-assisted radar system with its own data processing sub-system, providing a clutter free picture. Its excellent target acquisition capability allows it to detect and classify surface vessels and its multi-tracking capability enables it to operate at long range and cope with high sea states. An AQS-901 comprehensive, dual operator acoustics system analyzes and classifies contacts made by both passive and active sonobuoys. The CTS, which included the new Ferranti FIN 1012 INS for short range accuracy and Omega, replaced Loran for long-range navigation. The total digital computing capability of the Nimrod MR2 provided sixty times more computer and display power than was available on the MR1.

The prototype Nimrod XV147 was fitted with the MR2's navigation systems and CTS for development purposes and with this equipment fit flew for the first time on 15 April 1977. During the next two years XV147 was joined by three more MR2 development. For the programme all four aircraft flew almost 1,000 hours.

A programme for the conversion of thirty-five Nimrod MR1s to MR2 standard was set up at Woodford and the first aircraft, XV236, made its maiden flight after conversion on 13 February 1979 and was handed over to the RAF at a ceremony at Woodford on 23 August 1979. The programme was completed with the delivery of the last aircraft XV245 to Kinloss on 19 December 1985.

During 1979 it was decided that the existing colour scheme of white upper and grey lower surfaces was to be changed to hemp for the upper but retaining grey for the lower. This was introduced to reduce the visibility of the aircraft on the ground when viewed from the air. At the same time the 'tactical' national markings of red and blue, which left out the white, were introduced.

A major modification was designed early in the MR2 conversion programme to introduce the Loral Electronic Support Measures (ESM) to replace the existing Electronic Counter Measures (ECM). This new system was carried in pods mounted at the wing tips and required a new ESM/MAD operator's station. The ECM equipment was removed, leaving the large dielectric fairing on top of the fin surplus to requirements, although it was left in place to maintain aerodynamic integrity and to provide vacant space, if required, for any future development.

XV241 was selected as the development aircraft for the Loral ESM system and was delivered to Woodford in May 1978 where it was given a major service by BAe, who also installed instrumentation for monitoring the handling trials of the aircraft fitted with the ESM pods. After a test flight in March 1979 without pods, non-equipped ESM pods were fitted for aerodynamic assessment flight trials, which commenced in September 1979 and continued for the remainder of the year. On successful completion of these trials the pods were modified to represent the shape of the pods to be fitted to the Nimrod R.1 and the flight trials, with these modified pods were concluded in May 1980. XV241 was then fed into the MR2 conversion programme for conversion to MR2 standard and the complete installation of the Loral ESM system. Following completion of this work and the ESM ground trials XV241 made its initial flight in this configuration on 19 November 1982. BAe flight trials of the ESM system were followed by A&AEE C(A) release trials at Boscombe Down. Eventually, XV241 was returned to Woodford for refurbishment and preparation for delivery and was returned to service on 15 August 1986.

When only five MR2s had been delivered to the RAF, the Nimrod fleet suffered its first major accident, when the fourth MR2 XV256 crashed on 17 November 1980. The aircraft, which was carrying a crew of twenty, including five checking crew and an additional air engineer, flew into a dense flock of sea birds immediately after take-off from Kinloss, seriously damaging three engines and probably damaging the fourth. The aircraft crashed into the forest less than a mile from the end of the runway where it was destroyed by fire. Eighteen of the crew managed to escape from the wreckage, with some difficulty because of the fire, but the two pilots who had skilfully put the aircraft down in a controlled crash landing in the tree tops at minimum speed, saving the lives of the other crew members, were both killed. The captain of the aircraft, Flight Lieutenant Noel Anthony of the Royal Australian Air Force, was posthumously awarded the Air Force Cross and his co-pilot Flying Officer Stephen Belcher of the RAF received the Queen's Commendation for Valuable Services in the Air.

Early in the morning of 2 April 1982 a large Argentine invasion force landed on the Falkland Islands and, as the small detachment of Royal Marines based on the Islands were completely outnumbered, the Argentines had gained control before the end of the day. The British Government's response to this outrage was to order the preparation of a task force to sail to the South Atlantic to recover the Falkland Islands. The operation, given the name 'Corporate', was put under the overall command of Admiral Sir John Fieldhouse GCB. 'Corporate' was to involve thirty-three Royal Navy surface ships, six submarines, twenty-four Royal Fleet Auxiliaries, five trawlers and forty-five merchant ships. By the end of April some seventy ships had put to sea.

In order to provide maritime reconnaissance and search and rescue (SAR) cover, 18 (Maritime) Group ordered 42 Squadron at St Mawgan to deploy two Nimrod MR1s, three

XV147 at Woodford in August 1978 after an avionic update to enable it to be used as a prototype for the Nimrod MR2.

crews and the necessary ground crew to Wideawake, the USAF base on Ascension Island. On 5 April two Nimrods, XV244 and XV258, under the command of Wing Commander D.L. Baugh left the UK, arriving the following day at Ascension. The first operational sortie from Ascension was carried out by XV258 on 7 April. By mid-April the two MR1s had been replaced by two MR2s from RAF Kinloss, under the command of Wing Commander D. Emmerson, the commanding officer of 206 Squadron. This was, however, not quite the end of 42 Squadron's activities in support of 'Corporate', as they flew SAR patrols from St Mawgan, Freetown in Sierra Leone and Dakar in Senegal to cover Harrier flights to Ascension. Later in the year, after the Argentinean surrender, they also provided SAR cover from Wideawake for the Hercules transports flying to Port Stanley.

The lack of Air-to-Air Refuelling (AAR) restricted the use of the Nimrod over the vast area of the South Atlantic. Following a feasibility study the Procurement Executive of the Ministry of Defence issued British Aerospace at Woodford an instruction to proceed (ITP) with a modification introducing AAR on the Nimrod.

The ITP was issued on 14 April and the modification was designed, manufactured and installed in XV229, which made its initial flight with AAR on 27 April and was delivered to the RAF three days later for AAR training. An incredible achievement by the BAe team involved with the modification, although it must be admitted that Special Clearance for Service use, following joint BAe/A&AEE trials was issued rather than the normal C(A) Release. By 25 June, thirteen Nimrods, equipped with AAR had been delivered to the RAF. Nimrods fitted with AAR were designated Nimrod MR2Ps. The weapons system was also upgraded to carry two AGM-84A-1 Harpoon anti-shipping missiles, mounted in the weapons bay and as the Nimrods could possibly operate in enemy air-space, the defensive armament of four wing mounted AIM-9 Sidewinder air-to-air missiles was introduced.

With the benefit of AAR, XV232, flown by a crew from 201 Squadron, achieved an endurance record for operation Corporate when it made a long range reconnaissance flight which lasted nineteen hours and five minutes on 15 May and covered some 8,300 miles. Five days later the same aircraft, flown by a crew from 206 Squadron, covered 8,453 miles, but in the slightly shorter time of eighteen hours and five minutes. In all a total of 111 sorties were flown from Wideawake in support of Operation 'Corporate'. Operations continued after the Argentine surrender until 5 November, when the last Nimrod based on Ascension flown by 42 Squadron crews was providing SAR cover. It is understood that 51 Squadron, with its three electronic reconnaissance Nimrod R1s, did participate in Operation 'Corporate', but as one would expect details of its operations are never made public, so nothing is known of the actual part they played in 'Corporate'. It is known that one of the Nimrod R1s, XW664, was modified to give it AAR capability, but it was only returned to service at about the time of the Argentine surrender.

In the late 1960s a decision was made to phase out the Royal Navy's conventional, fixed-wing aircraft carriers, leaving the fleet with a serious gap in its air defence cover, following the loss of the Gannet AEW3s. To bridge this gap it was decided that the RAF would be responsible for the provision of Airborne Early Warning (AEW) cover, with aircraft operating from land bases. As an interim measure, twelve Shackleton MR2s were modified into AEW2s by the removal of the MR equipment and the installation of AN/APS20 radar that had been removed from the Gannets. These aircraft were to be operated by No.8 Squadron from RAF Lossiemouth, in the North of Scotland, although initially the Squadron reformed at Kinloss. It was expected that the Shackletons would be replaced by the Boeing E-3A AWACS or a development of the Nimrod by the end of the 1970s.

The Air Staff Target (AST) for an Airborne Early Warning Aircraft was issued in August 1972 and, following design feasibility studies, an Air Staff Requirement (ASR) was issued in February 1975. While Marconi-Elliott Avionic Systems Ltd worked on the development of the Mission System Avionics (MSA), HSA continued with the development of the Nimrod AEW airframe. At about this time the NATO nations, no doubt under some pressure from the U.S. Government, began to consider the Boeing E-3 AWACS as a standard AEW aircraft for a combined NATO force, with each of the nations bearing a proportion of the total cost. Although there was general agreement on the concept, after two years of negotiations the NATO defence ministers seemed unable to come to any agreement on the financial arrangements to procure an E-3 fleet. However, by 1977 the UK was desperate to make progress with a replacement for the Shackleton AEW 2 and so on 31 March 1977 Fred Mulley, the Secretary of State for Defence, announced that the UK was to proceed on its own with the Nimrod AEW, and the following day HSA received an ITP for the design, development and production of the Nimrod AEW.

Although some consideration was given to the use of an AWACS type rotordome on the Nimrod, it was dropped in favour of forward and rearward-looking radar mounted in the nose and tail of the aircraft. It was the large, bulbous radomes that were installed at the nose and tail to accommodate the radar scanners that were the most distinctive features of the Nimrod AEW. The original intention was that both the radomes were to be the same size and shape. However, wind tunnel trials showed the shape of the forward radome had to be more pointed to cope with bird strikes and rain erosion, with a more rounded radome at the rear to provide a stable break-away of the airflow. Due to its role the weapons bay was not required for weapons, so additional fuel tanks were installed in the bay for extra endurance and as it was no longer necessary to open the bomb doors in flight, so they were locked and could only be opened manually on the ground.

At the time of the issue of the ASR in 1975 a decision was made to modify a Comet for use as a development aircraft for the Mission Systems Avionics (MSA). For this purpose a Comet 4, XW626, which was being used as a flying laboratory by the Navigation and Radio Division of the A&AEE, was delivered to Woodford. XW626 had originally been delivered as a new aircraft, registered G-APDS to BOAC on 6 August 1959 and was operated by them, including periods

Nimrod MR1 XV241 fitted with non-equipped Electronic Support Measures (ESM) wing tip pods for ground resonance checks and flight trials for an aerodynamic assessment in 1979. XV241 was later brought up to full Nimrod MR2 standard, including the new ESM system. It was used by BAe for flight trials of the new system and later C(A) Release Trials by the A&AEE at Boscombe Down.

leased to Malaysian Airways, Air Ceylon and Kuwait Airways until it was taken out of service and sold to the MOA in January 1969. After modification at Woodford, including installation of a partial MSA and radar in a large radome in the nose but with no radar in the tail, XW626 made its first flight on 26 June 1977. The flight test programme continued at BAe and the RAE until XW626 made its last flight at RAE Bedford on 28 August 1981 and was relegated to training purposes at the Apprentice School. It was finally broken-up on 20 April 1994.

A total of eleven Nimrod AEW 3s were to be produced, all by conversion of existing airframes. The first three: XZ286, XZ287 and XZ281, were used as development aircraft, identified as Development Batch (DB) 1, DB 2 and DB 3. The first of these, XZ286, fully representative of the AEW externally, but without the MSA fit, made its maiden flight from Woodford on 16 July 1980 with BAe Manchester's chief test pilot Charles Masefield at the controls and was used for aircraft handling and performance trials. The remaining two development aircraft entered the flight programme during the next twelve months. In February 1979 Marconi-Elliott had a requirement for additional development trials, so it positioned DB2 and DB3 at Hatfield for the installation and commissioning of the MSA on these aircraft. It was intended that, when the development aircraft had completed their test flight programme, they were to be put onto the conversion track and brought up to full production standard for delivery to the RAF.

The first production Nimrod AEW 3, XZ285, was transferred off-track to the flight shed in December 1981 and flew for the first time on 9 March 1982 some fourteen months behind programme. Although design and development of the airframe were progressing satisfactorily, some of the slippage in the programme could be accounted for by industrial disputes at Woodford during 1977 and 1979. However, Marconi-Elliott Avionics Systems (subsequently GEC Avionics Ltd) were encountering serious problems with the development of their MSA and this had a knock on effect for HSA who had difficulty in obtaining design data to complete their work. Additionally, the MSA equipment racks were supplied by GEC eleven months behind programme. The MSA for XZ285 was finally delivered in January 1983 and the commissioning and clearing of the installation was carried out by GEC. XZ285 was cleared off-contract in August 1984 and, after a period of Joint Trials Unit (JTU) trials at Woodford, it was transferred to RAF Waddington on 18 December 1984. The JTU was a joint Ministry of Defence/Procurement Executive and RAF unit established to assess the servicing and operation of the Nimrod AEW3 in RAF service.

With the continuing problems with the MSA, British Aerospace (BAe) took advantage of the delays with the production aircraft by embodying outstanding modifications, including the AAR capability, which had been cleared on XV263, the third production AEW.

During 1983, the RAF had started to establish an AEW force headquarters at RAF Waddington, the former Vulcan base which was intended as the operational base for the Nimrod AEW3. Full training and maintenance facilities, including simulators and extensive workshops, were set up in readiness for the arrival of the aircraft, but in the event only three aircraft were delivered to the JTU at Waddington and none for operational service with the RAF.

The problems with the Nimrod AEW3 programme came to public notice towards the end of 1984 when stories started to appear in the press. It reached its peak when it became the subject of a BBC *Panorama* programme in February. By this time the programme had cost almost £1 billion and so every effort was made by MOD to get it back on track. By the end of 1985 there were rumours that it would be possible to start deliveries of Nimrod AEW 3s in 1988, but with the MSA performance some twenty-five percent below specification. However, in 1986, with ever escalating costs, not only of the Nimrod AEW programme, but also of keeping the No.8 Squadron's Shackleton AEW 2s in service well beyond their planned life had become too expensive. On 18 December 1986 George Younger, the Secretary of State for Defence, announced the cancellation of the Nimrod AEW programme, at a cost of £930 million and the cancellation of an order of six Boeing E-3A AWACS aircraft, at a cost of £860 million. A few days later MOD(PE) instructed BAe to prepare the three development aircraft and the remaining three production aircraft for transfer to Waddington at the earliest opportunity. The last flight of a Nimrod AEW 3 out of Woodford was made by the eighth production aircraft, XV261 on 14 July 1987. Most of the aircraft were subsequently delivered to RAF Abingdon for storage except for XV263, that was delivered to RAF Finningley as a ground instruction airframe and XZ282 that was delivered to RAF Kinloss on 14 September 1989 for spares recovery. This was the last flight ever made by a Nimrod AEW 3. Although it is understood that some of the Nimrod AEW 3 airframes had been offered to the research establishments for experimental use, none was ever used. By the end of 1995 they had all been broken up.

The Nimrod fleet suffered another major accident on 3 June 1984 when Nimrod MR 2 XV257 of 42 Squadron was scrambled on a tactical evaluation (Taceval) search and rescue (SAR) sortie, carrying a full crew of twelve and a Taceval umpire. Shortly after take-off from St Mawgan the weapons bay fire warning bell sounded and, after confirming that there was a fire, the captain transmitted a may-day call and turned back to base, landing some six minutes after take-off. All the crew evacuated the aircraft safely from the front door and the fire was quickly extinguished, although not before the rear section of the weapons bay was destroyed and the rear fuselage structure seriously damaged. The investigation into the incident showed that one of the eighteen 5in reconnaissance flares stowed at the rear of the weapons bay had dropped from its carrier and ignited when it struck the closed weapons bay doors. XV257 was subsequently patched up by a contractor's working party (CWP) provided by BAe and flown to Woodford on 7 November 1985 for category 4 repairs. However, after languishing at Woodford for many years it was decided not to proceed with the repair and the aircraft was scrapped in 1992.

On 16 May 1995 Nimrod R1 XW666 was on a routine, post-major service, air test from Kinloss when a fire broke out adjacent to No.4 (outer starboard) engine followed by one in No.3 engine. The crew carried out the engine fire drills, but were unable to extinguish or contain the fire, so the captain elected to ditch into the Moray Firth while he still had control of the aircraft. The ditching, four nautical miles north-east of RAF Lossiemouth, was successful and the crew of seven, the minimum Nimrod crew, escaped without serious injury.

The year 1995 was to prove most costly for the RAF's Nimrods. On 2 September 1995 XV239 coming to the end of its flying display at the Canadian International Airshow at Toronto and was making a left dumb-bell turn towards the display line when it stalled at low altitude and crashed into Lake Ontario. The aircraft sank immediately and none of the seven crew on board survived.

It was obvious that the loss of Nimrod R1 XW666, one of the three electronic reconnaissance aircraft operated by 51 Squadron, would have a significant effect on the squadron's operational capability. So within days the RAF had started to study the acquisition of a replacement. Because of the extreme urgency, an almost impossible timescale for the delivery of a replacement Nimrod R1 was decided upon. The project was named 'Anneka' after television presenter Anneka Rice who at the time was involved in the programme *Challenge Anneka* where she undertook apparently impossible projects, usually for charity. XV249, one of four Nimrod MR2s in storage at Kinloss, was selected for conversion and was immediately fed into the NMSU for a major service while the MOD(PE) negotiated a contract with BAe Aerostructures Ltd at Chadderton. It was returned to Woodford on 23 October 1995 where it was converted and was delivered to RAF Waddington on 19 December 1996. At Waddington all the specialized, electronic reconnaissance equipment was installed by the RAF's Electronic Warfare and Avionic Detachment (EWAD). XV249 made its first flight as a fully equipped Nimrod R1 on 2 April 1997 and after completion of the test flight programme and airborne calibration of the systems, 'Project Anneka' was declared complete on 28 April 1997.

With the primary structure of the Nimrod being virtually identical to the Comet, it was agreed that the results of the Comet fatigue test were acceptable for the Nimrod, confirming a design life in excess of the 10,000 hours demanded in the ASR. However, by the start of

Comet 4 XW626, originally G-APDS with BOAC, modified to include partial Mission Systems Avionics and the large, nose-mounted radome for the Nimrod AEW development programme. Flight trials with the aircraft commenced at Woodford in June 1977.

the Nimrod MR2 conversion programme it was apparent that with progressive increases in the weight of the aircraft, changes in the way the aircraft was operated and the possible affects of corrosion on the airframe it was decided to proceed with a full scale fatigue test at Woodford. During the conversion of XV227 to an MR2 a full suite of instrumentation was installed for the Nimrod Operational Flight Load Measurement Programme (NOFLMP). This aircraft, delivered to Kinloss on 2 December 1981 was flown on routine, operational flights to allow the measuring and recording of structural loading data, which was sent to Woodford for analysis. The results of this analysis were then used to produce a programme for the running of the fatigue test rig and subsequently, to ensure that the rig was in line with any changes in the operation of the Nimrod fleet.

The first prototype Nimrod, XV148, was selected as the test specimen, as it had just become available with the completion of the Searchwater radar development programme at RAE Bedford. XV148 was delivered to Woodford in March 1982, where the nose and tail was cut off, reducing the total length to 70ft and the wing structure was brought up to current modification standard. The airframe was then installed into a new computer controlled fatigue test rig in a building built specifically for the purpose. The testing continued over the next ten years, without any significant failures, confirming the fatigue life of the Nimrod fleet well into the twenty-first century.

Following the Iraqi invasion of Kuwait in 1990, three Nimrod MR2Ps left Kinloss on 26 August for Seeb in Oman. These Nimrods of the Kinloss Wing, operated by crews from 120, 201 and 206 Squadrons, were used for shipping surveillance in support of the United Nations naval blockade of Iraq. With the outbreak of the Gulf War, officially entitled Operation Granby by the British, the role of the Nimrod MR2s was changed to that of supporting the United States Navy's carrier groups. Additionally, throughout the conflict, Nimrods were on SAR stand-by in support of allied aircrew. Nimrod R1s of 51 Squadron operating from Akrotiri, Cyprus, flew their electronic surveillance missions in the area. The final Nimrod sorties for Operation Granby were flown in March 1991.

To improve the defensive capabilities of the Nimrod MR2s and R1s a series of modifications were introduced. These included wing mounted BOZ pods, which are countermeasure dispensers which dispense chaff (window) to break the radar lock of ground and airborne radar and also throws out infra-red decoys (IRD) to protect aircraft from IR heat seeking missiles. Also forward looking infra-red (FLIR) and a towed radar decoy (TRD) were introduced. These modifications, like those introduced for Operation Corporate, have been retained as standard fit on the Nimrods and have proved particularly invaluable during operations in the Adriatic, where Nimrods supported the UN blockades of Serbia and Montenegro in September 1992.

In 1960 the parents of Sergeant Nairn Fincastle Aird Whyte, who had been killed in action in 1943 while serving as an air gunner with Coastal Command, presented two trophies in memory of their son, to the RAF. Named as the Aird Whyte and Fincastle Trophies they became annual awards for maritime patrol competitions. The Aird Whyte Trophy was awarded to the Coastal Command and later 18 Group crew who achieved the best performance in anti-submarine warfare tests. The winning crew in the Aird Whyte competition then went forward to represent the RAF and his Squadron at the Fincastle competition against maritime crews of the Australian, Canadian and New Zealand air forces. Initially, Fincastle was simply a bombing competition with the competing crews operating from their home base and the results being sent to an adjudicating committee in London who analyzed the data and selected a winner. Starting in 1971, almost coincident with the Nimrod entering squadron service, the competition was completely revised to cover a wider range of ASW activities, with all the competing crews gathering at the same base, rotating on an annual basis between the four participating countries. The latest Fincastle Trophy held at Kinloss in 1999 was won by Flight Lieutenant Terry Woodward and his crew from 120 Squadron, RAF.

After completing the design and development of the Nimrod MR2 the design department started to prepare design proposals for a Nimrod mid-life update (MLU).

Nimrod AEW3, XZ286, with the very distinctive nose and tail radomes which provided 360 degree radar coverage. XZ286, identified as Development Batch (DB)1, was the first of three development aircraft used for the Nimrod AEW programme, flying for the first time on 16 July 1980. Although initially flying in the original Nimrod grey and white colour scheme, all the Nimrod AEWs were to have received the later hemp colour scheme before entering service.

However, before it had progressed very far, a major re-organization of BAe had resulted in the design of the MLU being transferred to the Military Aircraft Division at Warton. The plan was that Woodford was to concentrate on commercial aircraft with design and product support being provided for in-service aircraft by the Military Business Unit at BAe Chadderton. In the case of the Nimrod this was to continue up to the MLU when BAe Military Aircraft Division at Warton would take over design authority. The MLU was to have been a major equipment update with the introduction of a new acoustic processor and central tactical system. However, in May 1990 it was announced that the MLU was to be cancelled, on the recommendation of the MOD Equipment Procurement Committee and work was put in hand to prepare an Air Staff Target (AST) for a Nimrod replacement. Shortly afterwards the RAF had decided that they wanted the new Long-Range Air Anti-submarine Warfare Capability Aircraft (LRAACA), later known as the P-7A, being developed by Lockheed for the US Navy. On 20 July 1991 the P-7A project was cancelled by the US Navy, because of the very high cost forcing the RAF to look elsewhere for a Nimrod replacement.

The Nimrod MR2 replacement was covered by the Staff Requirement (Air) SRA420 for a replacement maritime patrol aircraft (RMPA) and by April 1992 consideration was being given to a version of the Lockheed P-3C Orion Update 3 and a Dassault Atlantique 2 fitted with an additional two jet engines mounted in pods under the wings. By early 1993 other projects had entered the competition. BAe was offering Nimrod 2000 a major rebuild and upgrade of the Nimrod MR2. Rather surprisingly, the Russians offered the Beriev BE-42 Mermaid twin-jet-engined amphibian. One of the schemes considered during the design studies for the Nimrod 2000 was the fitting of podded engines under the wings, instead of engines buried in the centre section. The change of thrust line would have required a very much larger tailplane. The scheme was soon dropped in favour of continuing with the existing Nimrod layout. In January 1995 MOD(PE) invited four potential prime contractors to tender for the supply of from twelve to twenty-five aircraft to SRA420. These included BAe, Dassault, Lockheed and a late addition to the list Loral supported by E-Systems and Marshall Aerospace. Loral's project, the Valkyrie was to be based on re-engined, refurbished and totally re-equipped ex-US Navy Lockheed P-3As and P-3Bs. These aircraft had already been taken out of service by the US Navy and were in storage.

Michael Portillo, the Secretary of State for Defence announced on 25 July 1996 that the Nimrod 2000 had been selected as the winner of the RMPA competition under SRA420. The contract, valued at around £1.8 billion, was to cover the conversion and major rebuild of twenty-one Nimrod MR2s. Basically, all that was to be retained of the MR2 was the fuselage, pannier skirts, fin, tailplane and elevators. The new, larger wing centre section, designed to take four of the newly developed 14,900lb thrust BMW Rolls-Royce BR710 engines, increased the wing span by 12ft to 127ft. The resulting increase in wing area restores the wing loading to that of the MR2 to compensate for the increased MRA4 take-off weight. The original plan had been to retain the existing outer wings, but it was later decided that new-build ones should be fitted. Other new components included the undercarriage, centre wing box, weapons bay doors, dorsal fin rudder and tailplane finlets.

The Nimrod 2000 later to be designated the Nimrod MRA4, will have the latest type, digital, 'glass' cockpit and be operated by a flight crew of two, following the elimination of the flight engineer. The new tactical command system is supplied by Boeing and integrated by GEC-Marconi and it is coupled with an effective and capable suite of sensors, including the new Searchwater 2000(MR) radar, supplied by Racal.

Initially the fuselages of the three Nimrods in store at Kinloss were delivered to FR Aviation at Bournemouth. The first, XV242, arrived at Bournemouth International Airport in the freight bay of a Heavylift Antonov AN-124 on 14 February 1997 and the remaining two were delivered over the following few days. The eighteen Nimrods required to make up the total contact quantity were to be flown from Kinloss to Bournemouth, as required, for the conversion programme. Up to five Nimrods were to be on the track in the large hangar at FRA, that had been built specifically for this programme. Following the structural rebuilding of the aircraft by FRA the green airframes were to be flown to BAe Warton for systems integration and flight testing.

The conversion programme proved to be much more complex than initially anticipated. In March 1999, when the programme had been running for just over two years, the Nimrod MRA4 Integrated Project Team Leader announced a delay of twenty-three months. BAE Systems at Warton hope to regain six months of the slippage by totally revising the conversion programme, cancelling the airframe structural refurbishment contract with FRA at Hurn and transferring the task to BAe at Woodford, the original home of the Nimrod. In addition, it is likely that the systems integration and the flight testing will also be carried out at Woodford rather than Warton. Towards the end of 1999 the first of the Nimrod MR2s for conversion arrived at Woodford from Kinloss, to be followed shortly afterwards by the first three partially completed fuselages, flown from Hurn inside Antonov An-124s, followed by the third fuselage early in 2000. The RAF hopes to achieve an operational capability with the Nimrod MRA4 early in 2005.

The Nimrod MRA4s will be, in effect, a new aircraft and as such will receive new serial numbers from the block ZJ514 to ZJ534, with a fatigue life in excess of twenty-five years. This

Nimrod R1 XV249, taking-off from Woodford on 19 December 1996 after completion of Project Anneka, the conversion of a Nimrod MR2 into a Nimrod R1 by BAe Aerostructures, as a replacement for XW666 which was written off when it ditched in the Moray Firth.

will mean that the RAF is likely to operate Nimrods continuously for a period of almost sixty years. However, when one considers that the Nimrod started life as the Maritime Comet, and that the Nimrod MRA4s will be flying with fuselages that were built on the original Comet 4 jigs at Chester, this will give the Comet a continuous history of some eighty years.

One
Comet Series 1 and 2

A wind tunnel model photographed during the DH106 design study stage on 10 August 1946. It shows the project to have highly swept wing and tail surfaces, following a very radical, early, tail-less design and before the more conventional design that was to enter production.

VW120, the last of the three experimental DH108 aircraft, with a Comet fuselage being manoeuvred in the background. The DH108, using the fuselage of a Vampire F1, was intended to gain knowledge of control of high speed tail-less aircraft for the proposed early tail-less DH106 design.

Airspeed Horsa II Glider TL348 fitted with a Comet shaped nose section to investigate visibility and the effect of rain. Alongside is the glider tug Handley Page Halifax VII PP389 which had previously been used by de Havilland for propeller development.

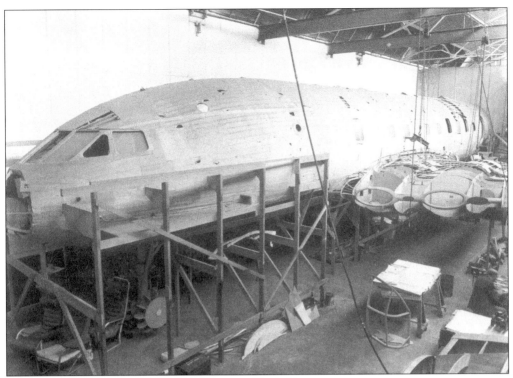

Here is the wooden mock-up of the Comet at Hatfield.

The first prototype Comet under construction at Hatfield.

The first prototype Comet, totally devoid of any identification markings, on engine runs at Hatfield during 1949. It later received the de Havilland 'B' condition identification G-5-1 before being registered G-ALVG.

Major Frank B Halford CBE FRAeS, Chairman and Technical Director of the de Havilland Engine Co. Ltd, Air Commodore Sir Frank Whittle, Sir Geoffrey de Havilland and Charles C. Walker CBE, AMICE Director and Chief Engineer of the de Havilland Aircraft Co. Ltd standing alongside the prototype Comet G-5-1 on 27 July 1949, the day of the first flight.

The Armstrong Whitworth AW55 Apollo G-AIYN, the DH106 Comet G-ALVG and the DH112 Venom FB1 VV612, three prototypes making their first appearances at the SBAC display at Farnborough in September 1949.

The second and third Comet 1s under construction at Hatfield in 1950. The second aircraft, 06002, was the second prototype G-ALYK and the third, 06003, was the first production Comet G-ALYP.

G-ALVG temporarily fitted with a four-wheel bogie main undercarriage, replacing the original, single, large wheel main undercarriage. The undercarriage bays were unable to accommodate the new undercarriage, so all flights were made with the undercarriage locked down. The bogie type undercarriage proved to be a significant improvement on the original and became standard on all the production Comets.

The second prototype Comet G-ALZK at Johannesburg in August 1951, when it was on loan to BOAC for route proving trials. The photograph shows clearly the original single wheel main undercarriage that was fitted to the two Comet prototypes.

A BOAC commemorative philatelic cover flown on the world's first scheduled passenger flight by a jet-powered airliner. The flight by the first production Comet 1 G-ALYP left London for Johannesburg on 2 May 1952.

G-ALYP at Tokyo in July 1952 during the first BOAC Comet route proving flight over the London to Tokyo route.

A BOAC flight crew at the controls of Comet 1 G-ALYS on 4 April 1952 during route proving trials to South Africa and the Middle East. The Comet flight deck was considered much simpler than an equivalent contemporary piston engined airliner. The captain is in the left-hand pilot's seat, the second officer in the right and behind them the flight engineer is on the right and the navigator on the left.

A family group of four in the luxurious eight seat forward compartment which was a standard feature of the thirty-six passenger layout of the BOAC Comet 1. The house of cards built by the little girl shows the virtually vibration free flight of the Comet.

A general view looking aft, of the rear twenty-eight seat cabin, showing clearly the comfort provided for the passengers by the 45in pitch of the seats.

The Comet production line at Hatfield in 1952. The Comet in the foreground is the first 1A for Canadian Pacific Airlines (CPA) which was registered CF-CUM, but before delivery was sold to BOAC and re-registered G-ANAV.

CPA's second Comet 1A CF-CUN, named *Empress of Hawaii*, outside the Comet Hangar at Hatfield in December 1952. Unfortunately, CF-CUN was destroyed in a take-off accident at Karachi on 3 March 1953 during the delivery flight to Sydney.

BOAC's only Comet 1A G-ANAV, previously CF-CUM of CPA, carrying the markings of both BOAC and South African Airways for service on the London to Johannesburg route.

The last of three UAT Comet 1As, F-BGSC, being manoeuvred out of the factory at Hatfield on 17 April 1953. To clear the low roof structure at Hatfield it was necessary to hold the tail down. F-BGSC was written-off in a landing accident at Dakar on 25 June 1953.

Comet 1A 5301 of the Royal Canadian Air Force (RCAF) Air Transport Command. This and the second 5302 were delivered to Canada in March and April 1953. The RCAF was the world's first air force to operate jet transports and also the first operator of jet airliners on the American Continent.

Air France's first Comet 1A F-BGNX on a flight from Hatfield on 8 June 1953. The fuselage of this aircraft is currently preserved in the Air France colour scheme by the de Havilland Aircraft Heritage Centre at Salisbury Hall.

Along with all the early civil Comets the two RCAF Comet 1As were withdrawn from service in 1954, but subsequently were delivered to de Havillands Chester for modification to Series 1XB standard. 5302 can be seen here on ground trials at Chester in 1957 after completion of the modifications. The main external change to the aircraft was the replacement of the rectangular windows with circular ones.

Comet 1XB G-AOJU on its delivery flight from Chester to Hatfield on 23 September 1957.
G-AOJU was converted from Air France Comet 1A F-BGNY to 1XB standard at Chester and
was subsequently re-identified as XM829 for use by the A&AEE at Boscombe Down.

The team of workers at Chester involved with the conversion of G-APAS in front of the
aircraft on 29 November 1957. G-APAS was the conversion of a second Air France Comet 1A,
F-BGNZ, to 1XB standard for the MOS.

Comet 1XB XM823, ex G-APAS, flying from Hatfield, when used by de Havilland Propellers Co Ltd for missile development. This aircraft, as G-APAS, is currently displayed at the Royal Air Force Museum, Cosford, in a BOAC colour scheme.

The sixth Comet 1 G-ALYT was converted on the production line to take four axial-flow Rolls-Royce Avon RA9 Mk501 turbo-jet engines in place of the DH Ghost engines, and was designated a Comet 2X, becoming in effect the prototype of the Comet 2. G-ALYT made its maiden flight at Hatfield on 16 February 1952.

54

The first production Comet 2 G-AMXA in final assembly at Hatfield on 24 July 1953. This aircraft was to have been the first of BOAC's order of eleven Comet 2s, but following the Comet disasters no Comet 2s were to enter commercial service.

The fuselage of Chester's first Comet being assembled on the track in May 1953. This aircraft, a Series 2, was allotted to UAT, but following the cancellation of the order after the Comet 1 disasters the fuselage was stored on the production track and was later completed as XK716 for the RAF. The high level of activity at Chester with Vampires, Venoms Doves and Herons in production is shown.

Chester's only Comet 2 XK716 on the production track in December 1956, along with two of the four Comet 1As that were converted into Comet 1XBs.

The increasing demand for the Comet 2 in 1952 to 1953 resulted in a third Comet production line being set up at Short's factory in Belfast. The photograph shows the fuselage of the first Short's-built Comet nearing completion in 1954.

Comet T2 XK669, one of two Comets that were initially used for crew training by 216 Squadron in 1956 and early 1957. The Comet T2s were subsequently brought up to full C2 standard by the introduction of a reinforced floor that was part of the C2 specification. XK669 was the second production Comet 2, originally flying in BOAC colours and bearing its civil registration G-AMXB for the first time on 3 November 1953 and after conversion into a T2 was delivered to 216 Squadron on 8 June 1956 and converted into a C2 the following year.

Comet T2 XK670 at Moscow Airport on 29 June 1956 waiting to return Nigel Birch the Minister of Transport and Civil Aviation after his official visit to Moscow.

De Havilland Chester's first Comet, a C2 XK716, awaiting delivery to Hatfield in May 1957 with D.H. Chester Flying Club's DH82A Tiger Moth G-ANTE parked alongside.

A line-up of five of 216 Squadron's Comet C2s at RAF Lyneham for the presentation of a standard to the Squadron on 24 May 1957.

Comet C2 XK698 *Pegasus* of 216 Squadron at RAF Lyneham in 1965. Delivered to the Squadron on 9 January 1957 it remained on their strength until it was retired in June 1967 to 27 MU at RAF Shawbury before being transferred to RAF St Athan, where identified as 8031M it was used as a ground instructional airframe.

Comet C2R XK663 was one of three Comet 2s converted for the RAF's electronic reconnaissance support role by Marshall's Flying School at Cambridge. Initially delivered to 192 Squadron at RAF Watton in 1957, the Squadron was reformed as 51 Squadron in August 1958 and XK663 remained in service until it was destroyed in a hangar fire at RAF Wyton on 3 June 1969.

Comet C2R XK695 was originally completed by de Havilland as a C2 and after four years service as a transport with 216 Squadron was converted to the electronic reconnaissance support role by Marshalls of Cambridge. XK695 was delivered to 51 Squadron on 8 March 1963 as a replacement for XK663. Although the first three Comet C2Rs had retained the original rectangular windows, restricting the aircraft to unpressurized operation, XK695 was to full C2 standard with thicker skins and circular windows.

G-AMXD, the first of two Comet 2Es flying in formation with the sole Comet 3 G-ANLO. The Comet 2Es were fitted with the improved Rolls-Royce Avon RA29 Mk524 engines intended for the Comet 4, in the outer engine bays and was used by BOAC for flight trials with the engines. In 1959, after completion of the BOAC trial, G-AMXD was transferred to the RAE at Farnborough as XN453 where it was used for long-range radio development trials until it was withdrawn from use in February 1973.

Two
Comet Series 3 and 4

The prototype Comet 3 G-ANLO being rolled-out at Hatfield on 25 March 1954. The fin and rudder were fitted when it was moved into the Comet Hangar.

BOAC ordered eleven Comet 3s and here the prototype, G-ANLO, is finished in BOAC livery. Despite a number of airlines showing interest in the Comet 3, de Havilland decided not to proceed to the production stage, but to use it for development of the projected Comet 4.

In December 1955 G-ANLO made a round-the-world flight. Here is at Bombay Airport on 3 December 1955, with an Air India Super Constellation. Air India had ordered two Comet 3s in 1953, but these were cancelled in 1954.

John Cunningham and Peter Bugge at the controls of G-ANLO in Hawaii during the around the world flight in December 1955.

Comet 3B G-ANLO finished in contemporary British European Airways (BEA) livery, and named *RMA William Brooks*, at the 1958 Farnborough Air Show. In 1957 G-ANLO was converted into the Comet 3B to act as the prototype of the Comet 4B, which was intended for the short to medium range role. The changes included reducing the wing span by 7ft and the removal of the wing pinion tanks.

The Comet 3B, with the serial number XP915, was transferred to the Blind Landing Experimental Unit (BLEU) at the RAE, Bedford in June 1961 for the development of autoland systems. Although XP915 was retired from flying in 1972, it was used the following year to test the effectiveness of urea formaldehyde foam to bring aircraft to a halt on the runway.

The first Comet 4, G-APDA, being prepared at Hatfield for its maiden flight on 27 April 1958. After use for development it was delivered to BOAC on 24 February 1959 and remained in service with them until it was sold to Malaysian Airways as 9M-AOA on 9 December 1965.

BOAC receiving its first two Comet 4s, G-APBD and G-APDC, at a formal ceremony at London Airport. The third production aircraft G-APDB is in the hangar and the fourth, G-APDC, is outside.

Three Comet 4s, including the Chester-built G-APDE on the left, and the Hatfield-built G-APDB in the centre of the BOAC maintenance hangar at London Airport.

Following page: A painting of a BOAC Comet 4, showing it shortly after take-off to emphasize its good short field performance, used by de Havilland as a cover for one of their Comet 4 sales brochures.

Chester's eighth Comet 4, G-APDR, being rolled out in July 1958. It was delivered to Hatfield on its first flight on 9 July 1959.

BOAC Comet 4 G-APDR on a test flight from Hatfield in July 1959. After service with BOAC it was sold to Mexicana as XA-NAZ in December 1964 and later re-registered XA-NAP. It was sold to Channel Airways in June 1971 as a source of spares and scrapped at Stansted in June 1972.

G-APDG was built out of sequence, after the original allotted airframe was used as the first Comet 4 LV-PLM for Aerolineas Argentinas. In the event G-APDG was BOAC's seventeenth Comet 4, delivered on 28 November 1959 and in December 1966 was sold to Kuwait Airways as 9K-ACI. Ahead of it is the first Comet 4C in Mexicana livery and temporarily carrying the British registration G-AOVU on the fin. It was delivered to Mexicana on 8 June 1960 carrying the registration XA-NAR and named *Golden Aztec*.

BOAC pilots at the controls of the first Comet 4 G-APDA. Like most contemporary airliners the Comet 4 was operated by a flight crew of four, two pilots, a navigator/radio operator and a flight engineer.

Meals being served to passengers in the first class cabin of a BOAC Comet 4.

The interior of a BOAC Comet 4 showing the very comfortable reclining seats and generous pitch of the seating in the first class cabin.

A number of BOAC Comet 4s were leased to various airlines. Here G-APDP appears in the BOAC colour scheme, but with Air Ceylon titles.

Comet 4 9M-AOB of Malaysian Airways. This Comet was originally BOAC's G-APDB until it was sold to Malaysia in December 1965.

Comet 4 XV814, of the RAE at Farnborough, was one of two Comets fitted with a Nimrod-type dorsal fin. Originally G-APDF of the BOAC fleet, it was bought by the RAE in March 1967 and used by them until January 1993 when it was transferred to the A&AEE for use as a source of spares for their Comet 4C, XS235. It was finally broken-up in August 1997.

Two of Dan Air's fleet of Comet 4s, G-APDK and G-APDP both originally with BOAC. Ultimately Dan Air was to acquire thirteen of BOAC's original fleet of nineteen Comet 4s.

Comet 4 G-APDE at Gatwick after it had been relegated to ground-training duties with the Dan Air Training Unit in the early 1970s.

The lower stub wing skin assembly being moved from the Stage 1 to the Stage 2 assembly jig. As can be seen these jigs were set in pits in the floor at Chester. Pits were a requirement for these jigs at Hatfield because of the low roof, but were not necessary at Chester with its very high roof.

LV-PLO, the second Comet 4 for Aerolineas Argentinas was named *Lucero de la Tarde* by the airline. Flying for the first time on 25 February 1959 it was delivered on 18 March 1959.

The Aerolineas Argentinas Comet 4 LV-PLO was re-registered LV-AHO in Argentina and was written-off on 20 February 1960 when it ran off the runway at Ezeiza Airport, Buenos Aires during crew training.

Five Comet 4s including two for Aerolineas Argentinas on the track at Chester in 1960.

Chester-built Comet 4 LV-PPA of Aerolineas Argentinas taking-off from Hatfield in July 1960. It was later re-registered LV-AHU and named *Centaurus*.

The first Comet 4B G-APMA, *Sir Edmund Halley*, of British European Airways (BEA) showing the lengthened fuselage and reduced span wings of the short to medium range version of the Comet 4.

Comet 4B G-ARGM at the Rolls-Royce airfield at Hucknall. G-ARGM was initially registered G-AREI, but was then re-registered to avoid confusion with the BEA Vickers Vanguard G-APEI.

G-APYC was the first of four Comet 4Bs ordered by Olympic Airways, the Greek National Airline. It was re-registered SX-DAK and named *Queen Frederica* on delivery to Greece.

This is Comet 4B G-ARGM of BEA Airtours, the inclusive tour airline based at Gatwick which BEA had formed in 1970 with ten Comet 4Bs.

Comet 4B, G-APZM, of Channel Airways, which had originally been SX-DAN of Olympic Airways. Channel Airways operated five Comet 4Bs from their base at Stansted Airport. All the aircraft were sold to Dan Air when the company ran into financial difficulties in 1972.

XA-NAS, the second Comet 4C for Mexicana, was delivered to Mexico on 14 January 1960.

A view of the Comet Hangar at Hatfield in 1960 containing an Aerolineas Argentinas Comet 4, a Mexicana Comet 4C G-ARBB (later XA-NAT), a BEA Comet 4B G-APMG and a MEA Comet 4C.

The first of two Comet 4s, VP-KPJ, ordered by East African Airways, and delivered to Nairobi Airport on 25 July 1960.

The mating of the fuselage to the wing of Comet 4C SU-ALD for Misrair, Egypt's national airline, in 1960. The high roof and extensive overhead crane system at Chester made it possible to lower the completed fuselage onto the wings.

Comet 4C SU-ALD of Misrair landing at Hatfield in June 1960.

The third Comet 4C, SU-ALE, of the United Arab Airlines (UAA), the re-titled Misrair on a test flight from Hatfield in December 1960. SU-ALE abandoned a take-off at Munich on 9 February 1970 and was written-off when it ran off the end of the runway.

UAA's name was later changed to Egyptair. Although initially the Comets retained the UAA livery, but with Egyptair titles, SU-AMV appears here in full Egyptair markings.

The first Comet 4C, OD-ADR, of Middle East Airlines (MEA) had initially registration OD-ADK allotted, although it was never taken up. Of the four Comet 4Cs operated by MEA three, including OD-ADR, were destroyed at Beirut Airport during a raid by Israeli forces.

The only Comet built specifically as a VIP transport was the luxuriously-furnished Comet 4C SA-R-7 for his Majesty King Ibn Saud of Saudi Arabia. It was delivered to the Saudi Royal Flight on 15 June 1962, but unfortunately after only a short time in service it crashed in the Alps on a flight from Geneva to Nice on 30 March1963, killing all on board.

Comet 4C ST-AAW was the first of two ordered by Sudan Airways. ST-AAW flew for the first time on 5 November 1962 and was delivered to the Sudan on 14 November. Both the Sudan Airways Comets were sold to Dan Air in June 1975.

9K-ACA, the first Comet 4C for Kuwait Airways first flew on 14 December 1962 at Chester and was delivered on 18 January1963. A second Comet 4C, 9K-ACE, was delivered in February 1964 and in December 1966 a Comet 4, G-APDG, was bought from BOAC and registered 9K-ACI.

XR395, the first of five of 216 Squadron's Comet C4s, is shown alongside a Bristol Britannia C1 of 99/511 Squadrons at RAF Lyneham.

In addition to their normal passenger role the RAF's Comet C4s could be converted to VIP or casualty evacuation roles. The photograph shows the forward cabin furnished for the VIP role.

All five Comet 4Cs awaiting disposal at 60 MU, RAF Leconfield shortly after the premature disbandment of 216 Squadron in June 1975. In September they had been sold to Dan Air.

G-BDIU, Comet 4C of Dan Air, one of the ex RAF C4s, XR396, at BAe Bitteswell on 9 July 1981, after its final flight with the Dan Air delivery crew comprising, Senior Engineer Officer Robin Durie, Captain John Waters and First Officer Peter Noonan. G-BDIU was dismantled at Bitteswell, with the cabin section of the fuselage going to Woodford for use as a mock-up for the Nimrod AEW programme and the nose section going to RAF Kinloss.

Comet 4 G-APDB, originally BOAC's second Comet 4, preserved in Dan Air livery by the Duxford Aviation Society at Duxford.

Comet 4C G-BDIX of Dan Air, originally the RAF's last Comet C4 XR399, preserved in Dan Air livery by the Museum of Flight, East Fortune, near Edinburgh and being used most effectively as a back-drop for a line-up of bubble cars. The aviation heritage of the three Messerschmitts on the right is clearly visible. They were designed by Fritz Fend, an ex-Messerschmitt aircraft designer, and constructed in the Messerschmitt factory at Regensburg.

Three

Nimrod MR Mk 1 and R Mk1

Comet 4C XV147 at Woodford following its maiden flight, a delivery flight of some forty miles from Chester on 25 October 1965. XV147 was allotted to the Nimrod programme for conversion into one of the two prototypes.

A reception party at Woodford to greet the crew of XV147 on its arrival at Woodford. Left to right they are Tommy A. House, Nimrod Project Manager; Gilbert Whitehead, Woodford Chief Designer; Jimmy Harrison, Woodford Chief Test Pilot; Pat Fillingham, Hatfield Assistant Chief Test Pilot and John Cunningham, Hatfield Chief Test Pilot.

XV147 on the track at Woodford for conversion into a Nimrod prototype during March 1966. Engine runs commenced on 28 June 1967 and it made its first flight on 31 July.

The Nimrod mock-up at Woodford in March 1966. In the background are Vulcan B2s on a refurbishment programme.

The prototype Nimrod XV147 on an early test flight from Woodford . XV147 was powered by four Rolls-Royce Avon 525B engines rather than the Spey engines used for all other Nimrods. The difference with the air intakes and depth of the centre section made it unrepresentative of the aerodynamics of the production Nimrod, so it was used primarily for systems development.

The last production Comet being converted into Nimrod prototype XV148 on the track at Chester on 18 July 1966. XV148 was fully representative of the Nimrod and was the first powered by Spey engines. In the foreground are two sets of HS125 wings.

Nimrod XV148 being rolled out at Chester in 1967.

Nimrod XV148 being prepared on the airfield at Chester for its delivery flight to Woodford.

XV148 on its maiden flight delivery from Chester to Woodford on 23 May 1967 with John Cunningham at the controls and Jimmy Harrison as co-pilot. Initially XV148 was flown without the distinctive MAD tail boom of the maritime reconnaissance Nimrods.

The Nimrod production line at Woodford in 1967 with the first production Nimrod MR1 XV226 in the foreground.

The first production Nimrod MR1, XV226, on its maiden flight from Woodford on 28 June 1968. The large dorsal fin was introduced to improve directional stability and had been tested on both the prototypes before being accepted for production.

A line-up of six Nimrods used for development at Woodford on 15 September 1969. The aircraft from left to right are XV230, XV234, XV231, XV229, XV228 and the prototype XV147.

Nimrod MR1 XV227 landing at Bitteswell on 23 April 1970 for the installation of bomb bay fuel tanks and preparation for the Squadron Mobility Role Conference. The aircraft was returned to Woodford in January 1971.

A Martel air to ground tactical strike missile installed under the port wing of the Nimrod prototype XV148 for trials by Hawker Siddeley Dynamics Ltd, Hatfield, on 4 July 1970.

Nimrod production at Woodford on 24 November 1970 with a total of ten Nimrods in production on two tracks.

The fifth production Nimrod MR1 XV230 was the first Nimrod delivered to the RAF on 2 October 1969 and was used by 236 OCU at RAF St Mawgan, Cornwall.

Nimrod MR1 XV235 after making its first flight on 13 February 1970 was delivered to RAF St Mawgan on 28 May for use by the two Nimrod units based there, 236 OCU and 42 Squadron.

Nimrod MR1 XV241 with the emblem of 201 Squadron, a seagull, wings elevated, painted on the dorsal fin, at RAF Kinloss on 14 June 1977. With the exception of 51 and 203 Squadrons it was exceptional for squadron markings to be carried by Nimrods and then only for commemorative purposes, squadron anniversaries, and participation in the Fincastle Trophy.

Nimrod MR1 XV234 of the RAF St Mawgan Wing flying over the nearby holiday resort of Newquay.

Nimrod MR1 XV249 flew for the first time on 22 December 1970 and was delivered to RAF Kinloss on 2 February 1971.

Included in the line-up at the Queen's Jubilee Review at RAF Finningley on 30 July 1977 was Nimrod MR1 XV250 with the 201 Squadron emblem on the dorsal fin. This was probably the only time that every Nimrod squadron had a Nimrod carrying its squadron markings at one time.

Nimrod MR1 XV259, bearing an octopus, the 206 Squadron emblem, on the dorsal fin at RAF Finningley for the Queen's Jubilee Review.

Nimrod MR1 XV249 with the winged seahorse emblem of the Malta based 203 Squadron at the Queen's Jubilee Review. 203 Squadron was the only Nimrod MR1 squadron to carry squadron markings permanently on all its aircraft and to have been permanently based overseas. Behind can be seen XV254 of 120 Squadron and XZ285 of 42 Squadron.

Nimrod MR1 XV246 incorrectly painted in a brown colour scheme, due to an error in the paint specification, on its final approach to RAF St Mawgan on 8 April 1977.

After re-painting in the correct NATO hemp colour scheme XV246 stands outside the Flight Sheds at Woodford on 14 June 1977.

The first electronic reconnaissance Nimrod R1 XW664, in its original grey and white colour scheme, was delivered to RAF Wyton for 51 Squadron on 6 July 1971. The main distinguishing, external feature of the R1 is the lack of the tail-mounted MAD boom.

Photographed at RAF Wyton early in 1991 Nimrod R1 XW666, finished in the current hemp colour scheme. It is fitted with an air-to-air refuelling probe, wing tip-mounted Loral electronic support measures (ESM) pods and BOZ countermeasures pods under the wings.

Nimrod R1 XW666 on its final approach to the runway at RAF Wyton in January 1991.

Nimrod R1 XW666 outside the 51 Squadron hangar at RAF Wyton on 5 September 1993.

Nimrod R1 XW665. The 51 Squadron emblem, a goose volant, designed for the Squadron by the artist and naturalist Sir Peter Scott, is carried on the dorsal fin.

A Nimrod R1 leading a formation of Canberras and Hawks in a flypast on the occasion of the closure of RAF Wyton for flying and its transfer to Logistics Command.

Nimrod R1 XW666 was ditched in the Moray Firth by a 51 Squadron crew when it suffered an engine fire while on an air test from the NMSU at RAF Kinloss on 16 May 1995. The ditching, four nautical miles north-east of RAF Lossiemouth, was successful with the crew of seven being rescued, while the aircraft broke its back and subsequently sank.

Nimrod MR2 XV249 was selected from the four Nimrods in storage at RAF Kinloss and is seen here being converted into a Nimrod R1, as Project Anneka in No.5 Hangar at BAe Woodford early in 1996.

After conversion Nimrod R1 XV249 on engine runs at Woodford.

Nimrod R1 XV249 taking-off for its first test flight at Woodford on 19 December 1996. The aircraft was subsequently delivered to RAF Waddington where the Electronic Warfare and Avionics Detachment (EWAD) installed the special equipment before it was handed over to 51 Squadron.

Four
Nimrod MR Mk 2

The first three production Nimrod MR2s, XV236, XV237, and XV255, on the conversion track at Woodford on 8 March 1979.

The first production Nimrod MR2 XV236 on a test flight from Woodford on 17 July 1979. It became the first MR2 to enter service when delivered to RAF Kinloss on 23 August 1979.

Nimrod MR2 XV228 flying over the coastline of Burghead Bay which is adjacent to RAF Kinloss.

The first two Nimrod MR2s, XV229 and XV238, fitted with air-to-air refuelling (AAR) probes, outside the Woodford flight sheds on 4 May 1982. The urgent requirement for Nimrods with AAR capability to take part in Operation 'Corporate', the Falklands Campaign, only succeeded because of almost superhuman activity at BAe Woodford. An Instruction to Proceed (ITP) was received from MOD(PE) on 14 April 1982 and the first Nimrod XV229, with AAR installed, flew for the first time on 27 April.

'Jane' – almost certainly the first example of Second World War style nose-art applied to a Nimrod. This artwork was apploed to the side of Nimrod MR2 XV234 of 201 Squadron by Flt Lt Neil Foggo during Operation 'Corporate', the Falklands Campaign in 1982.

Nimrod MR2 XV238 during AAR trials with Handley Page Victor K2 XH672.

Nimrod MR2 XV254 carrying four Sidewinder air-to-air missiles under the wings. Sidewinders were introduced initially to provide a defensive capability for Nimrods taking part in Operation Corporate.

A formation of three Nimrod MR2s, XV255, XV238 and XV232, flying over their base at RAF Kinloss.

Nimrod MR2 XV257 on the delivery flight from RAF St Mawgan to Woodford on 7 November 1985. Following the serious structural damage caused by the weapons bay fire on 3 June 1984, temporary repairs were carried out by a BAe contractors working party (CWP) at RAF St Mawgan. The aircraft was then flown to Woodford with the undercarriage locked down and cleared for a single flight. A contract for the repair of XV257 failed to materialize and in 1992 it was broken-up at Woodford.

A close-up view of the wing-tip pod containing Loral 1017A electronic support measures (ESM) equipment on a production Nimrod MR2 after having been cleared on the development aircraft XV241.

Nimrod MR2 XV231 fitted with Loral ESM pods, preparing for take-off at Woodford on 5 September 1985 after it had been major serviced by BAe at Woodford during 1985.

Nimrod MR2 XV258 fitted with Loral ESM pods, flew for the first time as a MR2 on 24 April 1985 and was delivered to Kinloss on 23 May.

Nimrod MR2 XV258 on finals for a landing.

Nimrod MR2P XV235 monitoring the meeting of two submarines at the North Pole. It has become an annual event for US and Royal Navy submarines to meet at the North Pole and teams from the two crews play a game of football on the ice.

Nimrod MR2P XV235 flying over the Scottish coast.

Nimrod MR2P XV241 flying along the coast of the Isle of Hoy in the Orkney Islands with the Old Man of Hoy to the right.

Nimrod MR2P XV235 flying over the Scottish Highlands.

Nimrod MR2P XV235 at Kinloss in 1991 with *Muscat Belle* nose art which had been applied for Operation Granby, the Gulf War.

Guernsey Girl nose art on what is believed to be XV258 taking part in Operation Granby. The subject of the artwork suggests that this Nimrod was being operated by 201 Squadron which has historic links with Guernsey.

XV232, one of two Nimrod MR2Ps of 206 Squadron taking part in the joint fleet exercise Joint Fleetex 98-1 at San Diego, USA. A Lockheed C5A Galaxy of the USAF can be seen taxiing behind it.

Group Captain Metcalfe, captain of the 42 (R) Squadron Nimrod MR2P XV243 en route to the FIDAE air show at Santiago, Chile in 1998. During its time in South America XV243 became involved in SAR activities when the all women crewed Royal & Sun Alliance catamaran lost its 103ft mast in heavy seas.

The co-pilot of XV243, Squadron Leader Taylor Devlin. The photograph shows the improved visibility from the flight deck with the increased depth of the windscreen panels and the eyebrow windows essential for low flying over the sea.

A crew member in position at the port beam lookout position.

Squadron Leader Ian Hampton at the Routine Navigator's station.

Wing Commander Sid Brown at the Tactical Navigators station. Behind him can be seen the Air Electronic Officer (AEO) at his station. The AEO is responsible for the two acoustic operators.

One of the Acoustic stations which are located along the starboard side of the cabin.

Nimrod MR2P XV245 over Ayers Rock, Queensland, Australia, in October 1998. This aircraft, operating from RAAF Edinburgh, was flown by a 206 Squadron crew as the reserve aircraft to XV231, the aircraft selected for the Fincastle Trophy Competition.

Nimrod MR2P XV260 was the eighth Nimrod to be converted into an MR2 and was delivered to Kinloss on 6 March 1981.

Nimrod MR2P XV228 carrying special markings on the fin and rudder to commemorate the Eightieth Anniversary of the formation of 42 Squadron.

Nimrod MR2 XZ284, one of two carrying special 206 Squadron markings on the fin and rudder, at Kinloss during 1996-1997.

The winning crew from 120 Squadron, after the Fincastle Trophy Competition held at RAF Kinloss during October 1999, in front of Nimrod MR2P XV254. The captain of the aircraft was Flt Lt Jerry Woodward.

The Nimrod prototype XV148 being manoeuvred into a new building on the Woodford Flight Shed site which had been specifically erected for the Nimrod full scale fatigue test.

XV148, the Structural Test Specimen (STS), installed in the computer controlled fatigue test rig. For this purpose the nose and tail had been removed, reducing the length of the fuselage to 70ft.

Five
Nimrod AEW Mk 3

Comet 4C XW626 (ex BOAC G-APDS) was converted by HSA for Airborne Early Warning (AEW) development. It was fitted with the front-mounted radome and early development mission systems avionics and a Nimrod type dorsal fin.

Nimrod AEW 3 conversion at Woodford on 18 July 1979. The aircraft in the foreground is the first development aircraft XZ286 (Development Batch (DB) 1).

The roll-out ceremony for the first Nimrod AEW3 XZ286 at Woodford on 30 April 1980.

The first production Nimrod AEW 3 XV285 taking-off from Woodford on its first flight on 9 March 1982.

The third production Nimrod AEW 3 XV263 was used by BAe for AAR development and was subsequently delivered to the Joint Trials Unit (JTU) at RAF Waddington on 20 December 1985.

Nimrod AEW 3 XZ286 after being brought up to production standard and repainted in the latest hemp colour scheme.

A Lossiemouth-based Shackleton AEW2 WR960 of 8 Squadron with one of its intended successors Nimrod AEW3 XZ285 breaking away after some formation flying for a publicity photographic shoot.

Six

Nimrod MRA 4 – the future

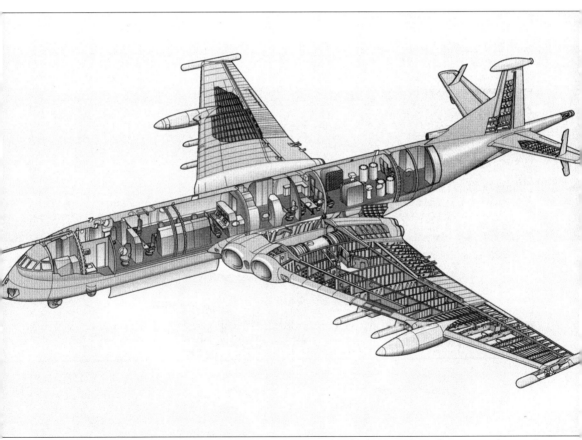

A cutaway illustration of the Nimrod MRA4, showing clearly the significantly increased size of the engine air intakes required for the BMW Rolls-Royce BR710 turbofan engines. Also clearly shown are the larger finlets on the tailplane.

The fuselage of the Nimrod prototype XV147 in 13 Hangar at BAe Warton, where it is used as a mock-up for the Nimrod MRA4 project.

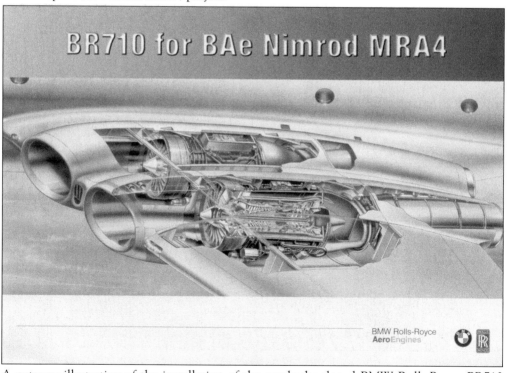

A cutaway illustration of the installation of the newly developed BMW Rolls-Royce BR710 turbofan engines in the Nimrod MRA4.

An artist's impression of the Nimrod MRA4 launching a Stingray homing torpedo from its weapons bay into a stormy sea.

The first Nimrod MR2 fuselage XV242, identified as DA3, in the Assembly Hangar at the Hurn -based FR Aviation on 3 June 1997. The Nimrod MRA4s have been allotted new serial numbers in the batch ZJ514 to ZJ534.

In 1999, with a slippage of nearly two years on the Nimrod MRA4 programme, the main conversion work was transferred from FRA to BAE Systems at Woodford. Here PA3 ZJ517 (originally XV242) is being unloaded at Woodford from the freight bay of an Heavylift Antonov AN124 on 16 December 1999 after a delivery flight from FRA at Hurn.

Three Nimrod MR2 fuselages including PA1, ZJ516 (XV247) and PA2, ZJ518 (XV234), at Woodford on 24 February 2000 awaiting conversion into MRA 4s.